RELIGIOUS DISSENT
IN THE MIDDLE AGES

MAJOR ISSUES IN HISTORY

Editor
C. WARREN HOLLISTER
University of California, Santa Barbara

William F. Church: *The Impact of Absolutism in France: National Experience under Richelieu, Mazarin, and Louis XIV*

Robert O. Collins: *The Partition of Africa: Illusion or Necessity*

J. B. Conacher: *The Emergence of Parliamentary Democracy in Britain in the Nineteenth Century*

Gerald D. Feldman: *German War Aims, 1914-1918: The Development of an Historical Debate*

Frank J. Frost: *Democracy and the Athenians*

Paul Hauben: *The Spanish Inquisition*

Bennett D. Hill: *Church and State in the Middle Ages*

Boyd H. Hill: *The Rise of the First Reich: Germany in the Tenth Century*

C. Warren Hollister: *The Impact of the Norman Conquest*

C. Warren Hollister: *The Twelfth-Century Renaissance*

Thomas M. Jones: *The Becket Controversy*

Tom B. Jones: *The Sumerian Problem*

Jeffry Kaplow: *France on the Eve of Revolution*

Archibald Lewis: *Islamic World and the West*

Anthony Molho: *Social and Economic Foundations of the Italian Renaissance*

E. W. Monter: *European Witchcraft*

Donald Queller: *The Latin Conquest of Constantinople* (in press)

Joachim Remak: *The First World War: Causes, Conduct, Consequences*

Jeffrey Russell: *Medieval Religious Dissent*

Max Salvadori: *European Liberalism*

Arthur J. Slavin: *Humanism, Reform, and Reformation*

W. Warren Wagar: *The Idea of Progress Since the Renaissance*

Bertie Wilkinson: *The Creation of the Medieval Parliament*

L. Pearce Williams: *Relativity Theory: Its Origins and Impact on Modern Thought*

Roger L. Williams: *The Commune of Paris, 1871*

RELIGIOUS DISSENT
IN THE MIDDLE AGES

EDITED BY
Jeffrey B. Russell
University of California
Riverside

John Wiley & Sons, Inc.
New York · London · Sydney · Toronto

Library of Congress Catalogue Card Number: 73-136722

Cloth: ISBN 0-471-74555-3
Paper: ISBN 0-471-74556-1

Printed in the United States of America

10 9 8 7 6 5 4 3 2 1

For Mark

SERIES PREFACE

The reading program in a history survey course traditionally has consisted of a large two-volume textbook and, perhaps, a book of readings. This simple reading program requires few decisions and little imagination on the instructor's part, and tends to encourage in the student the virtue of careful memorization. Such programs are by no means things of the past, but they certainly do not represent the wave of the future.

The reading program in survey courses at many colleges and universities today is far more complex. At the risk of over-simplification, and allowing for many exceptions and overlaps, it can be divided into four categories: (1) textbook, (2) original source readings, (3) specialized historical essays and interpretive studies, and (4) historical problems.

After obtaining an overview of the course subject matter (textbook), sampling the original sources, and being exposed to selective examples of excellent modern historical writing (historical essays), the student can turn to the crucial task of weighing various possible interpretations of major historical issues. It is at this point that memory gives way to creative critical thought. The "problems approach," in other words, is the intellectual climax of a thoughtfully conceived reading program and is, indeed, the most characteristic of all approaches to historical pedagogy among the newer generation of college and university teachers.

The historical problems books currently available are many and varied. Why add to this information explosion? Because the Wiley Major Issues Series constitutes an endeavor to produce something new that will respond to pedagogical needs thus far unmet. First, it is a series of individual volumes—one per problem. Many good teachers would much prefer to select their own historical issues rather than be tied to an inflexible sequence of issues imposed by a publisher and bound together between two covers. Second, the Wiley Major Issues Series is based on the idea of approaching the significant problems of history through a deft interweaving of primary sources and secondary analysis, fused together by the skill of a scholar-editor. It is felt that the essence of a historical issue cannot be satisfactorily probed either by placing a body of undigested source materials into the hands of inexperienced students or by limiting these students to the controversial literature of modern scholars who debate the meaning of sources the student never sees. This series approaches historical problems by exposing students to both the finest historical thinking on the issue and some of the evidence on which this thinking is based. This synthetic approach should prove far more fruitful than either the raw-source approach or the exclusively second-hand approach, for it combines the advantages—and avoids the serious disadvantages—of both.

Finally, the editors of the individual volumes in the Major Issues Series have been chosen from among the ablest scholars in their fields. Rather than faceless referees, they are historians who know their issues from the inside and, in most instances, have themselves contributed significantly to the relevant scholarly literature. It has been the editorial policy of this series to permit the editor-scholars of the individual volumes the widest possible latitude both in formulating their topics and in organizing their materials. Their scholarly competence has been unquestioningly respected; they have been encouraged to approach the problems as they see fit. The titles and themes of the series volumes have been suggested in nearly every case by the scholar-editors themselves. The criteria have been (1) that the issue be of relevance to undergraduate lecture courses in history, and (2) that it be an issue which the scholar-editor knows thoroughly and in which he has done creative work. And, in general, the second criterion has been given precedence over the first. In short, the question "What are the significant historical issues today?" has been answered not by general editors or sales departments but by the scholar-teachers who are responsible for these volumes.

University of California,   *C. Warren Hollister*
Santa Barbara

CONTENTS

Introduction   1

PART I:
Heresy and the Development of Doctrine   15

1. St. Paul, I Corinthians   17
2. St. Irenaeus, *Against the Heresies*   17
3. John Henry Newman, *Essay on the Development of Christian Doctrine*   19
4. Henry C. Bettenson: The Monophysite-Nestorian Controversy   22
5. Berengar of Tours: Augustin Fliche, *La Réforme grégorienne*   30
6. The Fourth Lateran Council: Henry J. Schroeder, *Disciplinary Decrees of the General Councils*   34

PART II:
Moral Controversies   35

7. Sigebert of Gembloux: Letter to Paschal II   37
8. The Pataria: Herbert Grundmann, *Ketzergeschichte des Mittelalters*   39
9. Valdes   41
   a. Raymonde Foreville and Jean Rousset de Pina, *Du Premier concile du Latran à l'avènement d'Innocent III*   41
   b. Bernard Gui, *Manuel de l'inquisiteur*   42
   c. Alan of Lille, *On the Catholic Faith*   52

PART III:

Radical Revolution: the Catharists   55

10. Summary of Catharist Beliefs: Jeffrey B. Russell, *Dissent and Reform*
                                                              57
11. The Heretics of Cologne   60
    a. Letter of Evervinus   60
    b. Eckbert of Schönau   63
12. Christine Thouzellier, *Catharisme et Valdéisme en Languedoc*   69
13. Antoine Dondaine, "La Hiérarchie cathare en Italie"   71
14. Antoine Dondaine, *Un Traité néo-manichéen du XIIIe siècle*   74

PART IV:

Heresy and Intellectual Movements   77

15. Abelard   79
    a. The Nineteen Capitula   79
    b. Letter of Saint Bernard   81
16. Amalric of Bena: *Contra Amaurianos*   83
17. Joachim of Flora: Gordon Leff, *Heresy in the Later Middle Ages*
                                                              84
18. Jeffrey B. Russell, "The Brethren of the Free Spirit"   86
19. William Cornelius: Thomas de Cantimpré, *De apibus*   91
20. William of Ockham: Gordon Leff, *Heresy in the Later Middle Ages*
                                                              92

PART V:

Late Medieval Heresy and the Reformation   97

21. Gordon Leff, "Heresy and the Decline of the Medieval Church"
                                                              99
22. John Wyclif
    a. Wyclif's Career: K. B. McFarlane, *The Origins of Religious Dissent in England*
                                                             114
    b. Wyclif's Beliefs: Tract by Wyclif   118
23. John Hus: Matthew Spinka, *John Hus*   123

PART VI:

Authority and Dissent 125

24. Lucius III, *Ad abolendam* 127
25. The Fourth Lateran Council: Henry J. Schroeder, *The Disciplinary Decrees of the General Councils* 128
26. Innocent III and the Heretics: Herbert Grundmann, *Ketzergeschichte des Mittelalters* 131
27. The Synod of Toulouse: Colman J. Barry, *Readings in Church History* 133
28. Secular Laws Against Heresy 135
    a. The Legislation of Frederick II: Henry Charles Lea, *A History of the Inquisition of the Middle Ages* 135
    b. The Sachsenspiegel: Edward P. Cheyney, *Original Sources of European History* 138

PART VII:

Personality, Society, and Dissent 139

29. Dissent and Millennarianism: Norman Cohn, *The Pursuit of the Millennium* 141
30. Marxist Interpretations: Ernst Werner and Martin Erbstösser, *Ideologische Probleme* 143
31. Idealist Interpretations: Ilarino da Milano, "Le Eresie medioevali" 147
32. Heresy at Florence: Marvin Becker, "Florentine Politics and the Diffusion of Heresy" 150
33. The Analysis of Collective Behavior: Neil Smelser, *Theory of Collective Behavior* 151
34. Conclusion: Gordon Leff, *Heresy in the Later Middle Ages* 158
Bibliography 159

RELIGIOUS DISSENT
IN THE MIDDLE AGES

INTRODUCTION

The Middle Ages were a period of unusually strong religious belief. In the ancient civilizations religion and politics were united and indistinguishable in their demands upon the public duty of the individual. During the Middle Ages this conception of the indivisibility of religion and public duty continued, but, far more than in classical Greece or Rome, religious concerns dominated and shaped political considerations. The idea of the *patria*, the "true native land," which for the Greeks and Romans had meant the *polis* or city, now in the Middle Ages meant heaven. The Christian was the citizen, not of an earthly republic, but of God's heavenly kingdom.

It is for this reason that medieval religious dissent is so significant. In the Middle Ages, to question or to deny the premises of Christian belief was to cut oneself off from the body of Christ and from the body of Christian society—it was to become, literally, a member of the body of Satan, corrupt and doomed. It was also, at least from the eleventh century, to put oneself in danger of life and limb, either before a secular or ecclesiastical tribunal or at the hands of a maddened mob. Knowingly to defy Christian orthodoxy was therefore an act either of enormous ignorance and folly or of great courage. It was a rejection not only of the religion but of the politics, the customs, and the decent opinion of one's neighbors and of the society in which one lived.

The study of religious dissent shapes our view of the Middle Ages. The Middle Ages were once supposed to be a time of monolithic faith: through religious dissent we catch sight, instead, of their wide diversity. Religious dissent illuminates the history of Christianity, proving that never, from the time of Constantine to the Reformation, as before and after, did Christianity cease to produce saints and martyrs and intellectuals and merchants and peasants as witnesses to its infinite richness and diversity. And the history of the opposition of dissent and orthodoxy is a sociological example of the ability of an institution—the

1

Church—to maintain over centuries an equilibrium between new ideas and internal consistency. The whole history of Western civilization is richer as a result of these confrontations in which the claims of Church and state, of individual conscience and the safety of society, of internal illumination and common assumptions, were so fruitfully debated.

The variety of medieval religious dissent is too great to admit of inclusive generalizations. But certain conflicts inherent in Christianity, or perhaps in all institutions founded on ideal principles, appear again and again. The simplest was the struggle of the spirit of change against the status quo. To those who used, as men always use, religion as a weapon with which to defend privilege and power, the dissenters replied that Christ had counseled the search for perfection. But among the forces of change and reform were two radically different spirits basing their arguments upon two very different gospel traditions: the tradition of prophecy and the tradition of order. The spirit of order was a spirit of conservative reform. The exponents of order argued that Christianity was a religion of radical transformation, a transformation of society into a society governed by justice, the right relationship between the laws of men and the laws of God. The spirit of prophecy was a spirit of radical reform, arguing that Jesus had taught the destruction of the old order, and the establishment, not merely of a better society, but of a whole new world, a transcendent kingdom of God. The exponents of prophecy were impatient of worldly change and demanded that men put away, immediately, the things of this world, that they leave nothing standing and go out naked into the desert where all horizons are open to God. The greatness of Christianity lies in these two tensions: first, between reform and the status quo, and second, between the reformers of prophecy and the reformers of order.

In the Middle Ages, Christians who disagreed with established authority were generally called heretics, from the Greek term *hairesis* (heresy). As used in the New Testament this term meant any kind of opinion or sect that was in disagreement with apostolic teaching. As the Church, during the first three centuries, attained more formal organization, heresy was formally defined as a persistent denial of Church doctrine. It has always been difficult to define precisely what is heresy and what is not. In the first place, the teaching of the Church has developed over the course of the centuries so that what may have been considered valid in one period is often considered heretical in the next. Secondly, even the most rigorous theologians or canon lawyers have found it difficult to define what is that core of the Church's teaching that can be considered so essential that to deny any part of it is heresy. Imagine a series of three concentric circles. Outside them all is that which cannot be considered Christian at all. The outermost circle consists of a number of widely held beliefs, more or less clearly defined. As time passes and these beliefs are discussed, some are rejected and relegated beyond the pale as heresy. Others are accepted more and more by the authorities in the Church and pass into the second circle: beliefs strongly and traditionally held by the Church. After further debate, sometimes for centuries, some of these beliefs were accepted into the inner core which no man might deny without ceasing to be a Catholic Christian. By any traditional criterion those who denied the inner core of doctrine were heretics, but it depended upon the temperament of the accuser whether denial of the beliefs of the second or third circles were deemed heresy.

Theologians in the Middle Ages were more inclined to assume that beliefs of the second and third level could not be challenged on pain of heresy than theologians are today. But even in the Middle Ages there was at no time a clear division between heresy and orthodoxy, for definitions varied according to time, place, and individual attitudes. Yet the historian must, at least for heuristic purposes, adopt a point of view. The most useful heuristic is to limit the field to Western Europe between the eighth and fifteenth centuries; i.e., to that territory under the religious domination of the Roman Catholic Church. Because the influence of the papacy was more predominant than any other ecclesiastical authority through most of the Middle Ages, it is reasonable to define as heretical for a given time beliefs so defined by the papacy at that time.

The historian, who, unlike the theologian, is less concerned with doctrinal truth in itself than with understanding the workings of society, will wish to examine what heresy is not only by narrow theological definition but also in relation to religious dissent in general. It is true that "religious dissent" is even harder to define than "heresy," but the use of the broader concept permits the historian to question why and how men and movements put themselves in opposition to the generally accepted beliefs and standards of their time and place. To give but one example, a certain Ramihrd was burned by the mob in 1077 at Cambrai for criticizing the immoral clergy. Ramihrd was merely saying in Cambrai what the new reform papacy was saying in Rome, but in conservative, backwater Cambrai, the program of papal reform had not yet been accepted, and Ramihrd's ideas shocked his auditors. Who then was the heretic? Ramihrd, condemned by the bishop as a heretic, or the bishop, who ignored papal teaching? A curious theological problem, and one that frequently arises again in the changing Catholic Church of the present era. But the historian will not want to belabor the question. He is concerned, not with affixing labels, but with explaining sociologically and psychologically both the bishop's resistance to Rome and Ramihrd's resistance to the bishop.

The history of Christian dissent is as old as Christianity itself. But, although all historical divisions are arbitrary, medieval dissent from about 700 to 1500 can be dealt with as a unit. Before 700, dissent was predominantly theological in content and clerical in personnel, the major exception to both generalizations being vague superstitions widespread among the illiterate bulk of the population. After 700, dissent was predominantly moral and lay. Medieval dissent ended with the Protestant Reformation, which wrought not only a chasm in the continuity of religion but also enormous political, economic, and social changes throughout European society.

Because of its primarily moral emphasis, medieval dissent is tied very closely to the perennial movements of reform within the Church that stirred with the mission of Saint Boniface in the eighth century, rose to a peak in the late eleventh and early twelfth centuries, and frequently reappeared in various forms thereafter. Medieval dissent was most often essentially religious in motivation and origin, rather than economic or specifically "social" in the sense of being connected with class, power, or status. There are some close correlations of dissent with social movements, particularly in the later Middle Ages, and sophisticated sociological analysis can elucidate, where the data are sufficient, the dynamics of dissent. But in general the history of medieval dissent is religious history, and a history specifically tied to reform movements in the Church at large.

The sources for the history of religious dissent are almost as varied as those for medieval history in general and include letters, papal pronouncements, conciliar decisions, penitentials (confessional codes specifying sins and their appropriate penances), saints' lives, poems, chronicles, and annals. The sources are sparse and laconic before the eleventh century. In that century they begin to be more numerous, and from the twelfth they become relatively rich.[1]

---

[1] For the sources, see the bibliography, particularly the works of Wakefield, Grundmann, and Russell.

Categories of Religious Dissent.   Six major categories of medieval religious dissent are distinguishable. The *Reformists* were the most numerous and important. Drawing their inspiration from the Gospels, they offered a radical moral criticism of the institutional Church and demanded a return to apostolic purity, apostolic poverty, and, often, what they believed was apostolic freedom from worldly authorities. As the Reformists responded to the reform movements by advancing beyond the limits of orthodoxy, the *Reactionaries* reacted by refusing to move fast enough and were consequently left behind by the forward movement of the Church. *Dualism* was imported into western Europe from the Balkans by Bulgarian missionaries in the 1140s. The dualists of western Europe are called Catharists (from *katharos*: pure); the Catharists of southern France were called Albigensians (from the town of Albi, one of their centers). Though most medieval dissent was centered on moral disputes, some were *intellectual and doctrinal heresies*, like adoptionism, the early scholastic controversies around the ideas of Abelard and Gilbert de la Porrée, and the late scholastic controversies around Siger of Brabant or William of Ockham. Many medieval people, like many people today, held ignorant or chaotic views, *eccentric heresies* that, if overtly expressed, would have been considered unorthodox by the authorities. Most of these people were inarticulate and left no records. Since their "errors" were not consciously unorthodox, they were not heretical in the strict theological sense; yet since superstitions were widely practiced and widely condemned, they are of interest to the historian concerned with the sociological and psychological bases of dissent. From the thirteenth century such beliefs were increasingly directed toward veneration of the Devil and formed the basis of the witch cults. In the earlier Middle Ages, occasional popular figures arose to take advantage of popular credulity to place themselves at the head of movements with occult or eccentric doctrines. A number of *peripheral varieties of dissent* also occurred: (1) doctrines that were in large part external and had little effect upon the West, like the Byzantine Iconoclasm of the eighth and ninth centuries; (2) apostate Christians who embraced Judaism or agnosticism; (3) and those who, partly in earnest or partly in jest, espoused the doctrines of courtly love or wrote anticlerical verse (whether or not they were in any formal sense "heretics" is less important than their mockery of established Christian values).

CHRONOLOGY

Medieval dissent as we have defined it began with the eighth-century reform movements introduced by Saint Boniface and other missionaries who founded schools and monasteries, pressed for moral renovation, and strengthened the organization and unity of the Church. Particularly in this early period, but even in the twelfth and thirteenth centuries, there are great numbers of vague references to heresy in the sources, some baseless rumors, others no doubt real but not specific enough to be very useful. The most important examples of dissent follow:

In the eighth century, many parts of western Europe were only superficially Christianized, so there are many examples of the practice of magic and other superstitions. An eccentric heretic named Aldebert[2] was condemned, along with an immoral priest named Clement, in the 740s. Saint Boniface struggled not only against this sort of corruption and superstition but also against what he took to be intellectual error, accusing the bishop of Salzburg, Vergil, of heresy for maintaining that the antipodes were inhabited. Toward the end of the century, Charlemagne and his contemporaries faced Adoptionism, a heresy strong in Spain and influential in France as well. Adoptionism, the doctrine that Jesus was born human and acquired divinity only at his baptism, was condemned by Charlemagne's Council of Frankfurt in 794. Also around the turn of the century, Frankish theologians led by Alcuin attempted, not wholly successfully, to find a middle ground between Byzantine Iconoclasm and its opponents who condemned it in the East at the Second Council of Nicea in 787. The Franks rejected Iconoclasm but feared that the Second Nicene Council had approved the worship of images as well as their veneration.

The effect of the Carolingian restoration of order and the consequent revival of intellectual activity was to heighten concern in the ninth century with intellectual and doctrinal matters. The Adoptionist and Iconoclast controversies continued into the ninth century, and then, toward midcentury, two long-lived disputes began. The

---

[2] For further references to any particular dissenting group or individual, see Walter Wakefield and Austin P. Evans, eds., *Heresies of the High Middle Ages* (New York, 1969). For dissenters before 1160, see Jeffrey B. Russell, *Dissent and Reform in the Early Middle Ages* (Berkeley and Los Angeles, 1965). For heretics 1200–1500, see Gordon Leff, *Heresy in the Later Middle Ages* (Manchester, 1967).

first was a debate on the nature of the eucharist between Paschasius Radbert, who upheld transubstantiation, and Ratramnus, who denied it. John Scotus Eriugena, called in to settle the argument, did not settle it. Eriugena in his treatise even seemed to skirt another heresy by arguing for predestination.[3] A monk named Gottschalk (b. ca. 800) was also accused of heresy for arguing in favor of predestination, though in fact Gottschalk's position was wholly consistent with that of Saint Augustine. Reformist dissent continued in the ninth century; witness Claudius of Turin, who died between 830 and 839; and the prophetess Theuda, an eccentric, who was active around 847 or 848.

The breakup of the Carolingian empire in the mid-ninth century and the renewal of invasions from without (Vikings, Magyars, Moslems) brought about a suspension of intellectual activity and an interruption of movements of reform. The sources become sparser, and coherent religious dissent, like other forms of cultural activity, seems to have declined drastically. Aside from a number of vague episodes, for example a few millennarian beliefs towards the end of the century (the importance of which was greatly exaggerated by many nineteenth-century writers), the only tenth-century dissent of note was that of Vilgard of Ravenna (active about 970–1000), who is alleged to have believed that the pagan authors appeared to him in spirit to teach him.

In the eleventh century, the revival of political and social stability permitted the revival of cultural activity, and both Intellectual and Reformist dissent reappeared, particularly after the middle of the century, when the movement of papal reform was under way.[4] Reformist dissent occurred frequently in the eleventh century.[5] The murder of Ramihrd at Cambrai in 1077 illustrates the resistance to the reform spirit, and throughout the latter part of the century Reactionary dissent was as prominent as that of the Reformists. Reformist heresy was not the only manifestation of extremism among

[3] Almost four hundred years after these controversies, in 1225, Pope Honorius III condemned several of Eriugena's propositions as pantheistic.

[4] The beginning of this movement may be dated 1048 with the accession of Pope Leo IX; its high point was probably the reign of Gregory VII, 1073–1085.

[5] At Cologne about 1000 (the Reformist is known only as "Citizen A"); Châlons-sur-Marne (Leutard) about 1000; Mainz in 1012; Orléans from 1015 to 1022; Limoges, Charroux, and Toulouse in the 1010s and 1020s; Arras and Liège, 1025; Monforte about 1028; Châlons-sur-Marne in the 1040s; Liège again between 1048–1054 (this dating is disputed—the incident may have occurred in the reign of Pope Lucius II, 1144–1145); Goslar in 1051; Milan (the Patarini) from 1057.

the reformers; the degree to which excessive zeal could go is illustrated by the bloody crusades of the eleventh and twelfth centuries directed not only against Moslems in Palestine but against Jews at home. Though Saint Bernard of Clairvaux declared that anyone who preached violence against the Jews was a heretic, there were vicious pogroms all over northwestern Europe, especially along the Rhine, significantly a center of the reform spirit. The incipient revival of theology and philosophy is responsible for the controversy surrounding Berengar of Tours (d. 1088). Berengar, in a way a "Reactionary" as well as an "Intellectual" heretic, upheld a conservative doctrine of the eucharist. This doctrine, that Christ was spiritually present in the eucharist but that the bread and wine were not physically transformed into the body and blood of Christ, had once been the common opinion of Christians, but as early as the ninth century Ratramnus had suffered for his denial of transubstantiation, and Berengar's refusal to accept this development of doctrine two centuries later earned him condemnation by no fewer than eleven synods.

The dissent of the first half of the twelfth century was characterized by a continuation of Reformism and by a growth of intellectual dissent, a product of the rapid growth of education and scholarship that had begun in the latter eleventh century. There were more and better schools now; new ideas or old ones newly revived were translated from Arabic and then Greek, and in the great schools of western Europe the method and content of scholasticism were being formed. The intellectual conservatism of men like Saint Bernard made them intolerant of the free speculations of scholars, and parts of the works of both Abelard (d. 1142) and Gilbert de la Porrée (d. 1154) were condemned as heretical. There were frequent occurrences of Reformism in the twelfth century.[6]

The difficulty of distinguishing orthodox from heretical reform, already apparent in the case of Ramihrd of Cambrai, again appears in the history of Lambert le Bègue of Liège and the movement of the Beguines he may have founded.[7] Lambert, who was born about

---

[6] At Ivois near Trier between 1102 and 1124; in the Low Countries (Tanchelm, d. ca. 1115); at Soissons (1114–1130); and Arras (1153). Albero of Mercke taught Reformism at Cologne about 1150; Peter of Bruys (d. between 1124 and 1140), Henry the Monk (d. ca. 1145), and Pons (1140s) preached Reformist doctrines in northern Europe, while Arnold of Brescia (d. 1154) spread revolutionary Reformism in Italy.

[7] The origin of the Beguines at Liège is strongly disputed. Herbert Grundmann argues that the term derived from Al*bigen*sian (Grundmann, *Religiöse Bewegungen im Mittelalter*, 2d ed. (Hildesheim, 1961), p. 181, n. 26).

1131, was a Liégeois priest of blameless life and apparently orthodox doctrine who was harrassed with accusations of heresy made by clergymen and others whose loose morals he had indicted. The Beghards and Beguines, who were laymen and women living a common life and practicing asceticism, became loosely connected in the next century with heretical movements like the Brethren of the Free Spirit and the *Apostolici*. Though it is not clear that the Beguines were ever really heretical, suspicions rose until at last they were condemned and proscribed by the Council of Vienne in 1311–1312. The Beguines in their motivation, goals, and way of life were very similar to the regular canons of the twelfth century and the Dominican and Franciscan friars of the thirteenth: all had in common the desire to preach a pure and simple life to the laity. Manifestations of eccentric dissent in the twelfth century included a strange occurrence at Sint Truiden in 1133–1136 and the career of Eudo of Brittany[8] (d. ca. 1148), who was condemned as a madman after arguing before a synod that he was the Son of God.

The landscape of dissent was radically altered around midcentury by the arrival of dualism, first imported in the 1140s into northern Italy and southern France by Bulgarian missionaries. Catharism spread rapidly through Europe: there were Catharists at Cologne by 1163 and at Oxford in 1166, for example, and in 1167 (or at least before 1172) there was a Catharist council at Saint-Félix de Caraman near Toulouse. Southern France now became the center of the heresy, although there were many Catharists in northern Italy, northern Spain, the Rhineland, and northern France as well. The Albigensians (Catharists of southern France) resisted all efforts to convert them by peaceful means, and from 1208 to 1213 a ruthless crusade, preached originally by Innocent III and then continued for political and personal profit by the kings and nobility of France, was waged against them. In spite of terrible losses, Catharism was not wholly destroyed, and there is evidence that it survived into the sixteenth century. There is a current revival of Catharism in southern France, but it lacks continuity with the original movement.

Though Catharism sometimes supplanted Reformism in certain localities, its overall effect seems to have been to encourage the growth of all heresies. Hugo Speroni, a jurist in the school of civil law at Bologna, became a Reformist heretic between 1177 and 1185; his followers were called Speronists. At Milan, the Reformist movement

[8] Incorrectly: Eon de l'Etoile.

of the Humiliati, which began about 1150, attracted much support. Most important of all was the movement begun by Valdes, who founded the "Poor Men of Lyon" between 1173 and 1178. Valdes was condemned as a heretic by Pope Lucius III and the Council of Verona in 1184 (where the Humiliati were also condemned), and he died between 1205 and 1218. But his followers, the Valdesians (Waldensians) preached all over western Europe and rivaled the Catharists in number and spirit. They began to decline in the late thirteenth century, although they were still fairly numerous in the fourteenth. Today, in northern Italy and Switzerland, there are still Waldensian churches validly boasting continuity to the present. In Lombardy in the latter half of the century appeared a peculiar sect, the Passagini, who taught Adoptionism and a return to the Mosaic Law.

With the growth and spread of a variety of sects, there were for the first time in the late twelfth and the thirteenth century really numerous groups of heretics. The result was the appearance, for the first time, of a formal institution of repression on the part of orthodoxy: the Inquisition. The Council of Verona in 1184 decreed that each bishop should inquire into the existence of heresy in his own diocese. This was no radical procedure but an extension on the one hand of the ancient episcopal duty of visitation and on the other of the inquest, a procedure of gaining information long employed by medieval kings. But in the thirteenth century Innocent III began, and Gregory IX developed, the papal Inquisition, which was to become a permanent institution with the title of the Holy Office and with the duty of seeking out and destroying heresy. Severe punishments were rare before the thirteenth century, though the first execution for heresy was ordered by King Robert the Pious of France at Orléans in 1022. The increasing severity of repression appears in the bull *Ad extirpanda* of Alexander IV in 1252, permitting Inquisitors the use of torture to secure confessions, and in secular legislation like the *De heretico comburendo* of Henry IV of England in 1401. The growth of heresy produced not only an increase of repressive measures but a great increase in the number of sources available to the historian, so that our knowledge of the heretics of the late twelfth through fifteenth centuries is much more detailed.

At the end of the twelfth and the beginning of the thirteenth century, there were a number of dissenters teaching partly intellectual, partly mystical doctrines that derived partly from Eriugena, and partly from the Arab philosopher Averroes and, through him, from neoplatonic pantheism. David of Dinant, an Averroistic, materialist pantheist, was condemned as a heretic in 1210. In the same year the writings of Amalric of Bena were also condemned. Amalric (d. 1206) was a professor at the University of Paris who taught a variety of intellectual pantheism derived from Eriugena. Amalric had a few followers, known as Amalricians, whose doctrines were strongly influenced by Joachim of Flora. Joachim (d. 1202) was a millennarian whose complicated metaphysics included the belief that there were three ages of the world: the age of God the Father, the age of the Son, in which we now live, and the third age, the age of the Holy Spirit, which was shortly to begin. In the third age, man, filled with the spirit, would create a kingdom of God on earth. The sect of the Ortlibians (Ortlib d. ca. 1200) were influenced by Amalrician-Joachist teaching. Later sects, like that of the Brethren of the Free Spirit, whose members were fairly numerous through much of the thirteenth century, combined Amalrician-Joachist with Reformist thought. The world was to be transformed by moral purity and love. The Brethren argued that the age of the Spirit had begun in their own time. God now dwelt within them and made them one with him. Accordingly they justified whatever they did as the will of God. The Guglielmites (the prophetess Guglielma died in 1282); the *Apostolici*, followers of Gerardo Segarelli; the followers of Brother Dolcino (d. 1327); the Italian sect of the Freedom of the Spirit; all of these arose out of the same mystical-Reformist milieu. Very close also to this milieu were the Fraticelli, Franciscans who refused to approve when the majority of the Order began to compromise the strict censures of St. Francis against personal possessions. The Fraticelli insisted upon asceticism to the point of Reformist heresy.[9] In the meanwhile, William Cornelius (d. 1245) and his followers in the Low Countries preached Reformist dissent. Toward the end of the century, an intellectual dispute led to allegations of heresy against Siger of Brabant (d. 1282), who taught that there were "two truths," a truth of reason and a truth of faith, the two being not necessarily compatible. Finally, towards the end of the century there appeared two manifestations of a deep trouble in the medieval spirit that was to grow in the next century: the Flagellants and the witch cults.

The fourteenth century was a time of severe economic and social change that encouraged radical cultural manifestations. A series of famines and plagues and a pronounced economic decline created

---

[9] Their most important leaders were Peter John Olivi (d. 1298), Ubertino da Casale (d. ca. 1330), and Angelo da Chiarino (d. 1337).

support for new and strange religious movements. The Flagellants roamed the roads nearly naked, singing, praying, and whipping one another; the witches transformed magic into a religious cult worshipping Satan; the Luciferans, influenced less by Satanism than by the antinomianism of the Free Spirit, argued grotesquely that the obscene or licentious act they practised was justified by the Holy Spirit within them. Another, more exalted, manifestation of the troubled spirit of the century was the rapid growth of mysticism. Here too the spirit of individual religion proved disquieting to the institutional Church, and parts of the writings of the greatest mystics, like Meister Eckhart (1260–1327), Heinrich Suso (ca. 1295–1365), and John Ruysbroeck (1293–1381) were declared heretical. Ruysbroeck was one of the founders of the Brethren of the Common Life, a group of laymen living a communal life and practising asceticism and individual prayer. The Turlupins practised apostolic poverty until they were outlawed by the Inquisition in 1372–1373. At the beginning of the century, William of Ockham's (d. 1327) skepticism about the ability of reason to understand God brought some allegations of heresy against him, just as they had been made against Siger of Brabant earlier. But William's thinking was still rooted in scholasticism. Closer to the end of the century appeared two intellectuals who wedded Reformist enthusiasm to an approach to theology that was simpler and more direct than that of the scholastics. John Wyclif (d. 1384), a professor at Oxford, had numerous followers called Lollards, who preached evangelical poverty in England, though their strength waned quickly after the first decades of the fifteenth century, largely owing to harsh measures taken against them by the government. Wyclif's teachings also influenced the Bohemian John (d. 1415), and the Husites in Bohemia and Germany, abetted by the Bohemian Brethren, followers of Chelcicky (d. 1460), had enormous success and influence in spite of, or perhaps partly because of, the execution of Hus himself at the Council of Constance. The evangelical doctrines of the Husites are the most direct precedent for the Protestant Reformation that in the next century transformed the limited kind of dissent typical of the Middle Ages into a revolution that shattered medieval Christendom.

HISTORIOGRAPHY[10]

From the Middle Ages themselves into the nineteenth century, writing about medieval dissent was almost wholly polemical, Catholics condemning it and Protestants hailing it as heralding the Protestant Reformation. Other historians interpreted it according to their own biases: for nineteenth-century liberals, the heretics were martyrs to freedom of thought; to Marxists they were heroes of the class struggle; they were even romanticized by the Nazis. Such tendentious interpretations still appear in the twentieth century, but they have been largely replaced by scrupulous attention to the sources on the one hand and interpretations based upon a sophisticated understanding of the context of religious and social history on the other.

In the nineteenth century exhaustive work in the sources was already being done by men like Ignaz von Döllinger in Germany and Henry Charles Lea in America. The twentieth century has seen the excellent work of men like Giovanni Gonnet in the Valdesian sources and Père Antoine Dondaine and Christine Thouzellier in the Valdesian and Catharist sources. Such excellent scholars as Raffaello Morghen, Ilarino da Milano, and Herbert Grundmann have turned their attention to working out new interpretations of dissent in the context of the history of medieval society. As a result of the great work of twentieth-century historians, a general consensus on some of the major issues is emerging: for example, it is now the general, though not universal, opinion of historians that Catharism was not indigenous to the West but was imported from the East, and that this importation came, not at the beginning of the eleventh century, but as late as the 1140s. But more problems and questions remain, and medieval dissent is a very rich field for the student to explore. One outstanding problem of interpretation is the question of whether the basic dynamic of dissent was provided by religious or by social and economic considerations. The sources are reticent on this question, and any answer depends in large part upon the student's general suppositions about historical causation. As in medieval history in general, there is still much original spadework on the sources to be done and

---

[10] The best bibliographies now available are in Wakefield and Evans and in Grundmann, *Bibliographie zur Ketzergeschichte des Mittelalters* (Rome, 1967). See also the notes in Russell, "Interpretations of the Origins of Medieval Heresy," *Mediaeval Studies*, XXV (1963), 26–53.

many monographs remain to be written. Yet answers of a sort can be provided by a sophisticated sociological and psychological analysis of the kind historians are now in a position to begin to make. The fact that historians now have so many new methods and so many new insights derived from the social sciences, from phenomenology, and from philosophy indicates that the great work to be done in the future is the reinterpretation of the materials we have in the light of this new knowledge.[11]

[11] For a short list of the most useful and most readily available works on medieval dissent, see the bibliography at the end of this volume.

PART I

Heresy and the Development of Doctrine

Until the middle of the nineteenth century most historians of Christianity were either convinced and traditional Protestants or convinced and traditional Catholics. Neither used a strictly historical approach to the problem of orthodoxy and dissent. Protestants tended to believe that the only true Christianity was that of the apostles and that the institutional Church of the Middle Ages was an unjustifiable perversion. The Protestants' difficulty, as it turned out, was deciding just what pure primitive Christianity was. The traditional Catholic approach was even more nonhistorical: it argued that in essentials the Catholic Church had never changed and was therefore essentially the same now as it was in the days of the apostles. The rallying cry of the Catholic traditionalists was the ancient saying of Saint Vincent of Lérins that Catholic doctrine was that which was believed always, everywhere, and by everyone. These nonhistorical interpretations had managed to keep afloat even through the seventeenth and eighteenth centuries when critical editions of the sources of Church history were being published which indicated the complexity of the history of doctrine. It was only in the nineteenth century, with the growth of historicism (the belief that all phenomena needed to be examined in the light of meaningful change), that Church historians achieved the necessary sophistication. It came to be recognized that the doctrines and institutions of the Christian Church had gradually developed, like other historical phenomena, over the centuries. Protestants might argue that much of the development was improper and Catholics that most of it was proper, but they could now agree with one another and with secular historians on a common historical approach.

In the light of this historical approach, heresy was seen to be an important component of the dynamics of developing doctrine. By stir-

15

ring up controversy and raising questions, heresies forced the Church to make decisions and define doctrine.

Heresy in the Middle Ages was more moral than doctrinal, but its action remained dialectical in nature. The great motive force for the development of the Church from the eighth through the fifteenth century was produced by the perennial movements of reform. These reform movements generated three general varieties of response: one moved with reform within the bounds of orthodoxy as an orthodox reformer, one was carried away by enthusiasm into heresy (the Reformists), or one resisted these movements to the point of being left behind in Reactionary heresy. This dialectic was powerful, but its components were seldom clearly defined. It is usually difficult to say when a person was so reactionary as actually to become a heretic, though there are some clear examples from the eleventh century in particular. And it is so difficult sometimes to distinguish the enthusiasm of the heretical Reformist from that of the orthodox reformer that the difference appears artificial and of little meaning to the student with historical, rather than theological, interests.

The tension between orthodoxy (which was defined by the institutional Church) and dissent (which was often the product of belief in personal inspiration by the Holy Spirit) has its ultimate origins in the ambivalence implicit in the teaching of Jesus on the Kingdom of God. Did Jesus mean by the Kingdom of God that salvation was possible through history, through a reform of this world, and accordingly found a Church to bear witness to his teaching through history? Or is the Kingdom of God attainable only by rejecting the world and being borne by the Spirit into that other, real world of God that stands in opposition to the essential corruption of "this world?"

1

St. Paul
I Corinthians

St. Paul himself predicted the function of dissent in the development of doctrine.

For there must be also heresies among you, that they which are approved may be made manifest among you.
SOURCE. I Corinthians xi, 19.

2

St. Irenaeus
Against the Heresies

St. Irenaeus (b. ca. 115), a Church Father, wrote a tract entitled Against the Heresies. *To the heretics, the Church too often resembled the "Prince of this World." For them, as for many orthodox ascetics, monks, and mystics, salvation came from withdrawal from this world and reliance upon the Spirit alone. But Irenaeus argues that the Church had the right and the duty to define doctrine. Without the institutional Church, the teachings of Christ would be lost.*

Irenaeus witnessed the conflict between the various schools [of theology] and the bishops as a whole. He reflected on the nature of their opposition, and this led him to consider both the source and content of Christian truth. First, what Irenaeus disputes is the authority of the heads of schools; their doctrine has no other basis but their own imagination, and what they are preaching is their own selves. When they claim to be the witnesses of an esoteric tradition, this assertion is false. In fact, they do not represent a tradition—each is the origin of his own doctrine. The ideas they put forward may be attrac-

SOURCE. I Corinthians xi, 19.
SOURCE. Jean Daniélou and Henri Marrou, *The Christian Centuries*, vol. 1, *The First Six Hundred Years*, Vincent Cronin, trans. (London: Darton, Longman & Todd Ltd; New York: McGraw-Hill, Inc., 1964), pp. 111–113. Reprinted by permission of the publishers.

tive, but they do not thereby possess any divine authority; they are merely human doctrines, creations of the intelligence.

Over against the heretical teachers Irenaeus sets the bishops. The bishops do not draw their authority from their own personal merits. They have been instituted and invested with an office which is to transmit a doctrine older than they are, and if we ask to whom this doctrine goes back, we see that it is to the Apostles, who instituted the first bishops. Irenaeus establishes that the episcopal succession clearly went back to the Apostles. He does what Hegesippus had tried to do, but draws on his own experience. So he establishes the succession of the three Churches he knows well: that of Smyrna, which goes back to John by way of Polycarp, that of Ephesus which goes back to Paul, and finally that of Rome, which goes back to Peter and Paul, and for which alone he gives the complete list of succession.

What we find in these lists of bishops is the tradition of the Apostles (*traditio ab apostolis*). The Gnostics also claim a link with the Apostles, but their tradition is without authority because it does not rest on the legitimate institution and transmission of authority; on the contrary, the bishops are heirs of the Apostles' authority and have the same authority for transmitting as the Apostles for teaching. What we find here in Irenaeus is a theology of ecclesiastical institution. The transmission of the Apostles' teaching is not left to the initiative of private teachers; the Apostles themselves established the organs by which they intended their teaching to be transmitted. These organs instituted by the Apostles are the only ones to possess the Apostles' authority; it is they alone who are the criteria of doctrines and guarantee their conformity with revelation.

Irenaeus sees confirmation of this in the unity of the bishops' teaching. Whereas the Gnostic schools are divided and contradict one another, the teaching of the bishops is one everywhere on earth. Here again Irenaeus's thought reflects the historical situation whose meaning it expresses. Nothing is more striking in the survey we have made than the swarm of sects, and doubtless for that reason our survey has been extensive and could be developed further. Facing them is the teaching of the bishops, the rule of faith contained in the Creed, in its simplicity and unity.

Irenaeus not only claims that this rule of faith exists, he develops its content. In contrast to the doctrines we have described, he unfolds the content of tradition. His work is essentially catechetical, whether it be the *Adversus Haereses* or the *Demonstration*. He does not claim to be an original theologian but sets forth the generally held doctrine;

his sources are chiefly catechetical tradition and scripture. But he expresses this doctrine with a profundity that shows its spiritual riches and itself provides evidence of divine authenticity. It is not for nothing that Irenaeus came from Asia, the land of charismata. His teaching is animated by the Spirit.

One characteristic gives his work a striking coherence, whether in his unfolding of the faith or in his formal study of it: unity. Unity characterizes the bishops' teaching over against that of the Gnostics; unity also characterizes the content of this teaching. The Gnostics shatter unity: they set in opposition God the saviour and God the creator, the invisible world and the pleroma of the aeons, the Old Testament and the New Alliance, the man Jesus and the Christ of the pleroma, the flesh and the spirit in man. In contrast, Irenaeus describes God's unity of design. One and the same God modelled the first Adam by his Word and Spirit, then in the fulness of time came to win back this man who belongs to him, in order to lead him to the accomplishment of his destiny.

The center of this theology is the "recapitulation" of all things in Christ. By this Irenaeus means first that man in his entirety is taken up by the Word and to man the Spirit communicates incorruptibility. But it is not only human nature, it is historic man with all his past, who is restored by the action of the Word. The unity of Christianity is the unity of a single plan by God. He begins with creation; sin spoils it, without destroying it; the Old Testament prepares mankind for the gift of the Spirit; in Christ the Word of God leads man to his fulfilment; the Spirit given in baptism makes every believer participate in this divine life.

3   *John Henry Newman*
           Essay on the Development of Christian Doctrine

John Henry Newman (1801–1890) was the most illustrious nineteenth-century English convert to Catholicism. His conversion was largely based upon his reading of history, from which he concluded that though Catholic doctrine had developed over the centuries it had not changed in essence. If Protestants were loath to accept his con-

SOURCE. John Henry Newman, *An Essay on the Development of Christian Doctrine* (1845; reprinted by Doubleday Image Books, 1960).

clusions, traditional Catholics were slow to accept the premise that doctrines had changed at all. Newman's argument was influenced by optimistic and evolutionary ideas drawn from nineteenth-century evolutionary thought as well as from the Augustinian view of history, and its impact on Church history, though late in coming, has been in the long run enormous.

I have been engaged in drawing out the positive and direct argument in proof of the intimate connection, or rather oneness, with primitive Apostolic teaching, of the body of doctrine known at this day by the name of Catholic, and professed substantially both by Eastern and Western Christendom. That faith is undeniably the historical continuation of the religious system, which bore the name of Catholic in the eighteenth century, in the seventeenth, in the sixteenth, and so back in every preceding century, till we arrive at the first—undeniably the successor, the representative, the heir of the religion of Cyprian, Basil, Ambrose, and Augustine. The only question that can be raised is whether the said Catholic faith, as now held, is logically, as well as historically, the representative of the ancient faith. This then is the subject, to which I have as yet addressed myself, and I have maintained that modern Catholicism is nothing else but simply the legitimate growth and complement, that is, the natural and necessary development, of the doctrine of the early church, and that its divine authority is included in the divinity of Christianity.

So far I have gone, but an important objection presents itself for distinct consideration. It may be said in answer to me that it is not enough that a certain large system of doctrine, such as that which goes by the name of Catholic, should admit of being referred to beliefs, opinions, and usages which prevailed among the first Christians, in order to my having a logical right to include a reception of the later teaching in the reception of the earlier; that an intellectual development may be in one sense natural, and yet untrue to its original, as diseases come of nature, yet are the destruction, or rather the negation of health; that the causes which stimulate the growth of ideas may also disturb and deform them; and that Christianity might indeed have been intended by its Divine Author for a wide expansion of the ideas proper to it, and yet this great benefit hindered by the evil birth of cognate errors which acted as its counterfeit; in a word, that what I have called developments in the Roman Church are nothing more or less than what used to be called her corruptions; and that new names do not destroy old grievances.

This is what may be said, and I acknowledge its force: it becomes necessary in consequence to assign certain characteristics of faithful developments, which none but faithful developments have, and the presence of which serves as a test to discriminate between them and corruptions. This I at once proceed to do, and I shall begin by determining what a corruption is, and why it cannot rightly be called, and how it differs from, a development.

To find then what a corruption or perversion of the truth is, let us inquire what the word means, when used literally of material substances. Now it is plain, first of all, that a corruption is a word attaching to organized matters only; a stone may be crushed to powder, but it cannot be corrupted. Corruption, on the contrary, is the breaking up of life preparatory to its termination. This resolution of a body into its component parts is the stage before its dissolution; it begins when life has reached its perfection, and it is the sequel, or rather the continuation, of that process towards perfection, being at the same time the reversal and undoing of what went before. Till this point of regression is reached, the body has a function of its own, and a direction and aim in its action, and a nature with laws; these it is now losing, and the traits and tokens of former years; and with them its vigor and powers of nutrition, of assimilation, and of self-reparation.

Taking this analogy as a guide, I venture to set down seven Notes of varying cogency, independence, and applicability, to discriminate healthy developments of an idea from its state of corruption and decay, as follows: There is no corruption if it retains one and the same type, the same principles, the same organization; if its beginnings anticipate its subsequent phases, and its later phenomena protect and subserve its earlier; if it has a power of assimilation and revival, and a vigorous action from first to last. On these tests I shall now enlarge, nearly in the order in which I have enumerated them.

[Newman's discussion of the first of these—preservation of type—is reproduced here as an example of his argument.]

FIRST NOTE OF A GENUINE DEVELOPMENT
PRESERVATION OF TYPE

This is readily suggested by the analogy of physical growth, which is such that the parts and proportions of the developed form, however altered, correspond to those which belong to its rudiments. The adult animal has the same make as it had on its birth; young birds do not grow into fishes, nor does the child degenerate into the brute, wild or domestic, of which he is by inheritance lord. Vincentius of Lerins adopts this illustration in distinct reference to Christian doctrine. "Let the soul's religion," he says, "imitate the law of the body, which, as years go on, develops indeed and opens out its due proportions, and yet remains identically what it was. Small are a baby's limbs, a youth's are larger, yet they are the same."

4   *Henry C. Bettenson*
The Monophysite—Nestorian Controversy

This is the perfect example of the way doctrinal dispute and heresy brought about the development of doctrine. The dispute began in the fourth century, when one Apollinarius began to teach that Christ had only one and one person: the divine. The reaction against Apollinarius caused Nestorius (patriarch of Constantinople from 428) to preach the opposite: that Christ had two natures and two persons: the human and the divine. The theologians of Alexandria, led by St. Cyril, now attacked the Nestorians and secured their condemnation at the ecumenical council of Ephesus in 431. However, the school of St. Cyril, particularly Eutyches and his followers, reacted to Nestorianism in an exaggerated fashion and stated the original position of Apollinarius even more bluntly. Thenceforward they became known as Monophysites ("Monophysis:" "one nature"). At the Council of Chalcedon in 451, Pope Leo I succeeded in securing the condemnation of both extreme groups and the definition of Christ as having one person but two natures (human and divine). The quarrel persisted for centuries, but the position of Chalcedon became the doctrine of the Catholic Church. It was a perfect example of a dialectical synthesis arising from a series of theses and antitheses.

The following selection consists of some of the documents regarding the dispute with commentary by Henry C. Bettenson.

By the end of the Arian controversy the true divinity and true humanity of Christ had been established as Catholic doctrine. Theological speculation was in the next century chiefly concerned with the problem of the mode of the union of deity and manhood. Three important heresies led to the Definition of Chalcedon.

SOURCE. Henry C. Bettenson, *Documents of the Christian Church*, 2nd ed. (London: Oxford University Press, 1963), pp. 63–73. Reprinted by permission of the publisher.

I. APOLLINARIANISM

Apollinarius, Bishop of Laodicea (d. 392), was a vigorous opponent of Arianism, and thus his teaching on the union of the two natures in Christ emphasized the divinity of our Lord at the expense of his full manhood. He held that In Christ the logos took the place of the human soul (i.e. the *rational* soul, or mind).

The opinions of A. have come down to us largely in fragments preserved by his critics, and in their representations.

An Examination of Apollinarianism
Gregory of Nazianzus, Archbishop of Constantinople

Do not let men deceive themselves and others by saying that the "Man of the Lord," which is the title they give to him who is rather "Our Lord and God," is without a human mind. We do not separate the Man from the Deity, no, we assert the dogma of the unity and identity of the person, who aforetime was not man but God, the only Son before all ages, who in these last days has assumed manhood also for our salvation; in his flesh passible, in his Deity impassible; in the body circumscribed, uncircumscribed in the Spirit; at once earthly and heavenly, tangible and intangible, comprehensible and incomprehensible; that by one and the same person, perfect man and perfect God, the whole humanity, fallen through sin, might be created anew.

If any one does not believe that holy Mary is the mother of God, he is cut off from the Deity. . . . If any assert that the manhood was fashioned and afterwards endued with the Deity, he also is to be condemned. . . . If any bring in the idea of two sons, one of God the Father, the other of the mother, may he lose his share in the adoption . . . . For the Godhead and the manhood are two natures, as are soul and body, but there are not two Sons or two Gods. . . . For both natures are one by the combination, the Godhead made man or the manhood deified, or whatever be the right expression. . . .

If any should say that the Deity worked in him by grace . . . but was not and is not united with him in essence . . . If any assert that he was . . . accounted worthy of sonship by adoption . . . If any say that his flesh came down from heaven and is not from hence, but is above us, not of us . . . (let him be anathema).

If any one has put his trust in him as a man without a human mind, he is himself devoid of mind and unworthy of salvation. For what he has not assumed he has not healed; it is what is united to his Deity that is saved. . . . Let them not grudge us our entire salvation, or endue the saviour only with the bones and nerves and appearance of humanity.

But, he urges, he could not contain two complete natures. Certainly not, if you are thinking of him physically. A bushel measure will not hold two bushels. . . . But if you will consider the mental and the incorporeal, bear in mind that in my one personality I can contain soul, reason, mind, and Holy Spirit. . . . If they rely on the text "The Word was made flesh". . . they do not realize that such expressions are used by *synecdoche*, whereby the part stands for the whole.

Apollinarianism was condemned at a synod at Alexandria, 362, by synods at Rome under Damasus, and at Constantinople, 381.

II. NESTORIANISM

a. *The Anathemas of Cyril of Alexandria*
Cyril, Bishop of Alexandria, 412–444

The controversy began in 428 with Nestorius' objection to the ascription to the Virgin of the title Θεοτόκοσ ("God-bearer," not so startling as the English "Mother of God," the Greek stressing the Deity of the Son rather than the privilege of the mother). The title had been commonly used, at least since Origen, and the "Alexandrians" were quick to see the implications of his contention. Cyril secured the condemnation of Nestorius by a Synod at Rome, Aug. 430; ratified the sentence at a synod at Alexandria, and sent to Constantinople a long letter expounding his doctrine and ending with the twelve anathemas.

1. If anyone does not acknowledge that Emmanuel is in truth God, and that the holy Virgin is, in consequence, "Theotokos," for she brought forth after the flesh the Word of God who has become flesh, let him be anathema.

2. If any one does not acknowledge that the Word which is from God the Father was personally united with flesh, and with his own flesh is one Christ, that is, one and the same God and man together, let him be anathema.

3. If any one in the one Christ divides the persons after their union, conjoining them with a mere conjunction in accordance with worth, or a conjunction effected by authority or power, instead of a combination according to a union of natures, let him be anathema.

4. If any one distributes between two characters or persons the expressions used about Christ in the gospels, etc . . . . applying some to the man, conceived of separately, apart from the Word, . . . others exclusively to the Word . . . , let him be anathema.

5. If any one presumes to call Christ a "God-bearing man" . . . , let him be anathema.

6. If any one presumes to call the Word, the God or Lord of Christ . . . , let him be anathema.

7. If any one says that Jesus as man was operated by God, the Word, and that the "glory of the only-begotten" was attached to him, as something existing apart from himself . . . , let him be anathema.

8. If anyone presumes to say that "the man who was assumed is to be worshipped together with the Divine Word" . . . , let him be anathema.

9. If any one says that the one Lord Jesus Christ was glorified by the Spirit, as if he exercised a power alien to himself which came to him through the Spirit . . . , let him be anathema.

12. If any one does not confess that the Word of God suffered in the flesh and was crucified in the flesh . . . , let him be anathema.

This letter, with the anathemas, was approved at the Council of Ephesus in 431.

b. *Cyril's Exposition*
Cyril

This "Dogmatic Letter" (the "Second letter to Nestorius"), Feb. 430, was read and approved at Ephesus and later at Chalcedon. The later letter with the anathemas (above) was not formally sanctioned at Chalcedon.

. . . We do not [in saying the Word "was incarnate," etc.] assert that there was any change in the nature of the Word when it became flesh, or that it was transformed into an entire man, consisting of soul and body; but we say that the Word, in a manner indescribable and inconceivable, united personally to himself flesh animated with a reasonable soul, and thus became man and was called the Son of man. And this was not by a mere act of will or favor, nor simply adopting a role. The natures which were brought together to form a true unity were different; but out of both is one Christ and one Son. We do not mean that the difference of the natures is annihilated by reason of this union; but rather that the Deity and Manhood, by their inexpressible and inexplicable concurrence into unity, have produced for us the one Lord and Son Jesus Christ. It is in this sense that he is said to have been born also after a woman's flesh, though he existed and was begotten from the Father before all ages. . . . It was not that an ordinary man was first born of the holy Virgin, and that afterwards the Word descended upon him. He was united with the flesh in the womb itself, and thus is said to have undergone a birth after the flesh, inasmuch as he made his own the birth of his own flesh.

In the same way we say that he "suffered and rose again." We do not mean that God the Word suffered in his Deity . . . for the Deity is impassible because it is incorporeal. But the body which had become his own body suffered these things, and therefore, he himself is said to have suffered them for us. The impassible was in the body which suffered.

In the same way we speak of his death. . . .

Thus it is one Christ and Lord that we acknowledge, and as one and the same we worship him, not as a man with the addition of the Word . . . because the body of the Lord is not alien from the Lord; and it is with this body that he sits at the Father's right hand. . . .

We must not then separate the one Lord Christ into two Sons. Some who do this make a show of acknowledging a union of persons; but this does not avail to restore their doctrine to soundness. For Scripture does not say "the Word united to himself the person of a man," but "the Word was made flesh." And that means precisely this, that he became partaker of flesh and blood, just as we do, and made our body his own. He was born of a woman; but he did not cast aside his being God and his having been begotten of God the Father. He assumed our flesh; but he continued to be what he was. . . .

III. EUTYCHIANISM

In 433 a creed of union was drawn up to reconcile the Alexandrine and Antiochene views, "Theotokos" was admitted, and "union" used instead of "conjunction". But neither party was really satisfied, and the Alexandrians, who were troubled at what seemed to them an excessive insistence on the distinction of the two natures, were ready, after the death of Cyril, to support the extreme "Alexandrianism" of Eutyches, an elderly monk of Constantinople, whose anti-Nestorian zeal far outran his imperceptible theological discretion. In November 448 he was summoned to attend a synod at Constantinople to answer charges of heresy.

a. *The Admissions of Eutyches*

Flavian (Archbp. of Const.). Do you acknowledge Christ to be of two natures?

Eutyches. I have never yet presumed to speculate about the nature of my God, the Lord of heaven and earth; I admit that I have never said that he is consubstantial with us. . . . I confess that the holy Virgin is consubstantial with us, and that of her our God was incarnate. . . .

Florentius. Since the mother is consubstantial with us, then surely the Son is also?

E. Please observe that I have not said that the body of a man became the body of God, but the body was human, and the Lord was incarnate of the Virgin. If you wish me to add that his body is consubstantial with ours, I will do so; but I take the word consubstantial in such a way as not to deny that he is the Son of God. Hitherto I have altogether avoided the phrase "consubstantial after the flesh." But I will use it now, since your Holiness demands it. . . .

Florentius. Do you or do you not admit that our Lord who is of the Virgin is consubtantial [with us] and of two natures after the incarnation?

E. . . . I admit that our Lord was of two natures before the union, but after the union one nature. . . . I follow the doctrine of the blessed Cyril and the holy fathers and the holy Athanasius. They speak of two natures before the union, but after the union and incarnation they speak of one nature not two.

Eutyches was condemned, and appealed to Leo, Bishop of Rome, who upheld Flavian. But the Emperor Theodosius II called a Council at Ephesus under the presidency of Dioscorus, successor to Cyril in the see of Alexandria and heir to all that was worst in Cyril's character and methods of theological controversy, and at the "Robber Council," 449, Eutyches was upheld and Flavian deposed. But Theodosius died in 450 and in the next year the Council of Chalcedon approved the "Tome of Leo" and formulated the "Chalcedonian Definition."

b. *The Tome of Pope Leo the Great*

"Peter has spoken through Leo. This is the teaching of Cyril. Anathema to him that believes otherwise" (the bishops at Chalcedon). Leo addressed himself to the following points:

I. [Eutyches' foolishness and misunderstanding of Scripture]
II. He did not realize what he ought to hold concerning the in-

carnation of the Word of God, and he had not the will to seek out the light of understanding by diligent study in the wide range of Holy Scripture. But he might at least have received with careful hearing that common and universal confession, in which the whole body of the faithful acknowledge their belief in GOD THE FATHER ALMIGHTY AND IN JESUS CHRIST HIS ONLY SON OUR LORD WHO WAS BORN OF THE HOLY GHOST AND THE VIRGIN MARY. For by these three statements the devices of almost all heretics are overthrown. God is believed to be both Almighty and Father; it follows that the Son is shown to be co-eternal with him, differing in no respect from the Father. For he was born God of God, Almighty of Almighty, co-eternal of eternal; not later in time, not inferior in power, not dissimilar in glory, not divided in essence. The same only-begotten, eternal Son of the eternal Father was born of the Holy Ghost and the Virgin Mary. But this birth in time has taken nothing from, and added nothing to, that divine eternal nativity, but has bestowed itself wholly on the restoration of man, who had been deceived: that it might overcome death and by its own virtue overthrow the devil who had the power of death. For we could not overcome the author of sin and death, unless he had taken our nature and made it his own, whom sin could not defile nor death retain, since he was conceived of the Holy Spirit, in the womb of his Virgin Mother, whose virginity remained entire in his birth as in his conception. . . . That birth, uniquely marvellous and marvellously unique, ought not to be understood in such a way as to preclude the distinctive properties of the kind [i.e. of humanity] through the new mode of creation. For it is true that the Holy Spirit gave fruitfulness to the Virgin, but the reality of his body was received from her body. . . .

III. Thus the properties of each nature and substance were preserved entire, and came together to form one person. Humility was assumed by majesty, weakness by strength, mortality by eternity; and to pay the debt that we had incurred, an inviolable nature was united to a nature that can suffer. And so, to fulfil the conditions of our healing, the man Jesus Christ, one and the same mediator between God and man, was able to die in respect of the one, unable to die in respect of the other.

Thus there was born true God in the entire and perfect nature of true man, complete in his own properties, complete in ours. By "ours" I mean those which the Creator formed in us at the beginning, which he assumed in order to restore; for in the Saviour there was no trace of the properties which the deceiver brought in, and which man, being deceived, allowed to enter. He did not become partaker of our sins because he entered into fellowship with human infirmities. He assumed the form of a servant without the stain of sin, making the human properties greater, but not detracting from the divine. For that "emptying of himself," whereby the invisible rendered himself visible, and the Creator and Lord of all willed to be a mortal, was a condescension of compassion, not a failure of power. Accordingly, he who made man, while he remained in the form of God, was himself made man in the form of a servant. Each nature preserves its own characteristics without diminution, so that the form of a servant does not detract from the form of God.

The devil boasted that man, deceived by his guile, had been deprived of the divine gifts and, stripped of the dower of immortality, had incurred the stern sentence of death; that he himself had found some consolation in his plight from having a companion in sin. He boasted too that God, because justice required it, had changed his purpose in respect of man whom he had created in such honor, therefore there was need of a dispensation for God to carry out his hidden plan, that the unchangeable God, whose will cannot be deprived of its own mercy, might accomplish the first design of his affection towards us by a more secret mystery; and that man, driven into sin by the devil's wicked craftiness, should not perish contrary to the purpose of God.

IV. The Son of God therefore came down from his throne in heaven without withdrawing from his Father's glory, and entered this lower world, born after a new order, by a new mode of birth. After a new order, inasmuch as he is invisible in his own nature, and he became visible in ours; he is incomprehensible and he willed to be comprehended; continuing to be before time he began to exist in time. . . . By a new mode of birth, inasmuch as virginity inviolate which knew not the desire of the flesh supplied the material of flesh. From his mother the Lord took nature, not sin. Jesus Christ was born from a virgin's womb, by a miraculous birth. And yet his nature is not on that account unlike to ours, for he that is true God is also true man. There is no unreality in this unity since the humility of the manhood and the majesty of the deity are alternated. For just as the God [deity] is not changed by his compassion, so the man [manhood] is not swallowed up by the dignity [of the Godhead]. Each nature [form, sc. of God and of servant] performs its proper functions in communion with the other; the Word performs what pertains to the Word, the flesh what pertains to the flesh. The one is resplendent with miracles, the other submits to insults. The Word withdraws not from his equality with the Father's glory; the flesh does not desert the nature of our kind. . . . And so it does not belong to the same nature to say "I and the Father are one" and "The Father is greater than I." For although in the Lord Jesus Christ there is one person of God and man, yet the source of the contumely which both share is distinct from the source of the glory which they also share. . . .

c. *The Definition of Chalcedon*, 451

Therefore, following the holy Fathers, we all with one accord teach men to acknowledge one and the same Son, our Lord Jesus Christ, at once complete in Godhead and complete in manhood, truly God and truly man, consisting also of a reasonable soul and body; of one substance with the Father as regards his Godhead, and at the same time of one substance with us as regards his manhood; like us in all respects, apart from sin; as regards his Godhead, begotten of the Father before the ages, but yet as regards his manhood begotten, for us men and for our salvation, of Mary the Virgin, the God-bearer; one and the same Christ, Son, Lord, Only-begotten, recognized IN TWO NATURES, WITHOUT CONFUSION, WITHOUT CHANGE, WITHOUT DIVISION, WITHOUT SEPARATION; the distinction of natures being in no way annulled by the union, but rather the characteristics of each nature being preserved and coming together to form one person and subsistence, not as parted or separated into two persons, but one and the same Son and Only-begotten God the Word, Lord Jesus Christ; even as the prophets from earliest times spoke of him, and our Lord Jesus Christ himself taught us, and the creed of the Fathers has handed down to us.

5   *Berengar of Tours*

One of the perennial questions of the Church concerned the eucharist. All Christians were agreed that Christ was truly present in the consecrated bread and wine of the Mass, but there was no agreement as to the manner in which this was true. Various

SOURCE. Augustin Fliche, *La Réforme grégorienne et la reconquête chrétienne* (Paris: Librairie Bloud & Gay, 1950) pp. 106–109. Translated for this volume by Jeffrey B. Russell. Reprinted by permission of the publisher.

points of view were held in the early Church, but in the ninth century the issue began to come to a head. Those who believed in a physical change in the bread and wine by virtue of the consecration came slowly to predominate and eventually to achieve the definition of their position as doctrine. In the ninth century it was still possible to argue against transubstantiation and remain orthodox; by the eleventh century Berengar of Tours was condemned as a heretic for so arguing, and the Fourth Lateran Council of 1215 formally defined transubstantiation as Catholic doctrine. The question was revived at the time of the Protestant Reformation.

For a long time Pope Gregory VII had known about this scholar, whose theories about the eucharist went against the teachings of the Church. It was Gregory himself, who in 1054, before he became pope, had presided over the Council of Tours, where Berengar had appeared. And it was Gregory who afterwards had ordered that incautious scholar to go to Rome in order to explain his teachings before Pope Leo IX. Gregory had acted with leniency and had sincerely wished to bring to an end a debate which was becoming dangerous for the Church. The death of Pope Leo IX, however, meant that it was necessary to put off the visit to Rome, and it was only during the pontificate of Nicholas II that Berengar was able finally to undertake the journey that Hildebrand had suggested. In April 1059 he appeared before a synod at the Lateran.

The result of his appearance was completely different from that which the future Gregory VII had wished. Instead of yielding, Berengar attempted to justify his ideas, and as a result he was met by indignant counterarguments on the part of certain members of the council. Finally the council forced him to sign a retraction, drawn up by Cardinal Humbert of Silva Candida, which he read before the council after having solemnly burned his writings in the presence of the bishops, giving them his oath that he would not again fall into his previous errors.

Everyone believed that Berengar was sincere, and the successor of Nicholas II, Alexander II, kept him under his protection. Protection was necessary. After the death of his protector, Geoffrey Martel, Count of Anjou, on November 14, 1060, Berengar, who had returned to Angers where he had functioned as an archdeacon, was subject to violent attacks on the part of the new count, Geoffrey the Bearded. Geoffrey tried to drive Berengar from the diocese, and it appears that the archdeacon was obliged to give up his office. To what extent the accusations that were pressed against him were wellfounded is difficult to say. The bishop of Tours resisted the demands of the count and refused to condemn Berengar formally. According to Bernold of Constance, Berengar had circulated a protest against the condemnation of his eucharistic beliefs by the Lateran synod. Some historians have doubted Bernold on the grounds that if what he said had really been true it is surprising that Berengar would have complained to the pope that he was being persecuted and even more surprising that Alexander II would have intervened energetically on his behalf. They doubt that the pope would have sided with him against his attackers and reproved the count for not having obeyed the papal orders that had been sent to him by legates. Berengar claimed that the pope even threatened the count with anathema if he should fail to stop his attack against a man (Berengar) whose great Christian love made him worthy of great consideration, and that the pope ordered the archbishop of Tours and the bishop of Angers to do everything in their power to protect Berengar from being molested by the count. Recently it has been demonstrated that all of the alleged pontifical letters used by Berengar were false and that he had probably forged them himself; Alexander II, therefore, apparently did not intervene in the controversies in Anjou which continued after his death.

In a treatise entitled *A Book on the Body and Blood of the Lord Against Berengar of Tours*, which was composed between 1066 and 1070, Lanfranc accused Berengar of having misunderstood the Fathers whom he quoted and even of voluntarily distorting their meaning. Berengar replied by his *Treatise on the Holy Mass Against Lanfranc*. Though he did not dare to publish the treatise right away, he there revealed his own position completely: he did not hesitate to cast doubts on the infallibility of the Church; he denied that councils had any authority; he attacked both Pope Nicholas II and Pope Leo IX; and he claimed that he had confidence in nothing but the Holy Scriptures, and the Holy Scriptures freely interpreted. The violence of these arguments led up to a new crisis which broke out during the reign of Gregory VII. The question of Berengar came up again at a council held at Poitiers on January 13, 1076, with the papal legate Gerald presiding. The heresiarch apparently appeared before this assembly, where he was nearly killed by the enraged mob. It is not clear what happened after that. Gregory VII asked Berengar to keep quiet, and Berengar had an interview with Hugh of Die (the papal legate) in 1077 at the time of the Council of Dijon, but the legate gave him a cool reception, which decided him to return to Rome in order to work out some kind of understanding with the pope himself. The lack of sources makes it impossible to describe the interview: Gregory VII hardly mentioned Berengar in a letter of May 7, 1078 to Hugh of Cluny. . . .

It is probable, however, that it had just been decided that Berengar was to appear before the next synod of Rome, which took place on February 11, 1079. The text of the oath that the heretic read in front of this assembly has been preserved. He affirmed that he believed— in his heart as well as on his lips—that the bread and the wine of the altar became by virtue of consecration the true flesh and the true blood of Christ born of the Virgin . . . and not just as a sacramental sign, but in their true properties and substance.

Gregory VII was obliged to accept this apparent submission of Berengar, who, it appears, continued to play a double game. It is noteworthy that the alleged Bull of February 1079 that anathematized all those who harmed or treated as a heretic the former scholar of Tours, and the letter of 1080 by which Archbishop Raoul of Tours and Bishop Eusèbe of Angers were asked to defend Berengar against Count Fulk of Poitiers, do not appear in the Papal Register. These too may have been forged by the heretic.

This may explain the attitude of Berengar, who in a letter written at the end of 1079 or at the beginning of 1080 declared that his oath had once again been forced from him and that he had been driven to act against his own conscience. He was forced to appear before a council, this time in Bordeaux in the beginning of October 1080. There in the presence of the legates Amatus of Oléron and Hugh of Die, of Archbishop Gozelin of Bordeaux and of Archbishop Raoul of Tours, he retracted his errors. Subsequently he seems to have kept quiet, and he died a few years later.

However, the movement that he had begun did not die with him. At the Council of Piacenza in March 1095 Urban II again condemned Berengar's thesis on the eucharist and solemnly proclaimed that after consecration the bread and the wine of the altar are not merely a sign of Christ, but really his body and blood. It thus does not appear that the faith had been seriously shaken. By the moderation which he had always shown in regard to Berengar, even while retaining his firmness on the doctrine of the eucharist, Gregory VII . . . saved the Church from a violent doctrinal dispute.

6   *Henry J. Schroeder*
              Disciplinary Decrees of the General Councils

The following formal proclamation of transubstantiation as the doctrine of the Church was made at the Fourth Lateran Council of 1215 under the presidency of Pope Innocent III.

There is one Universal Church of the faithful, outside of which there is absolutely no salvation. In which there is the same priest and sacrifice, Jesus Christ, whose body and blood are truly contained in the sacrament of the altar under the forms of bread and wine; the bread being changed (*transubstantiatio*) by divine power into the body, and the wine into the blood, so that to realize the mystery of unity we may receive of Him what He has received of us. And this sacrament no one can effect except the priest who has been duly ordained in accordance with the keys of the Church, which Jesus Christ Himself gave to the Apostles and their successors.

SOURCE. Henry J. Schroeder, O.P., trans., *Disciplinary Decrees of the General Councils* (St. Louis: Herder, 1937). Reprinted in Colman J. Barry, *Readings in Church History* (Westminster, Md.: Newman Press, 1960), vol. I, p. 439. Reprinted by permission of the Newman Press.

PART II
Moral Controversies

Medieval heresy was more often moral than intellectual in nature. The reform movements in the Church produced a double reaction. Some men responded so enthusiastically to reform that their enthusiasm carried them to ascetic extremes and often heresy—these were the Reformists. Others resisted reform and sometimes accused the papal reformers of promoting Reformist heresy. These extreme conservatives were left behind by the developing moral doctrine of the Church and were often themselves designated as heretics—these were the Reactionaries.

7   *Sigebert of Gembloux*
                     Letter to Paschal II

Sigebert of Gembloux, a writer of Liège, whose bishop, Otbert, strongly supported the Emperor against the reform papacy, wrote a letter to Pope Paschal II (1099–1118). In the letter he accused the popes of promoting heresy with their new doctrines and praised the imperialists for holding to the ancient tradition of the Church.

Why are we called false clerics, when we live according to the canons and when we are worthy by our works to be called clerics? I tell you that a man who wishes to exclude us from the people of God is not, not I say, a man of God. Mother Church, you have not nurtured us in order that we might be called false clerics. Since you have dismissed us against our will, we cannot call you our mother. It is astounding how our Lord Paschal has listened to false reproaches, seeming to accept at face value the accusations which are so easily poured forth against us. At one time he calls us excommunicate, and at another he emotionally calls us false clerics. As readily as the heart of David the King brought forth good words, the heart of Lord Paschal spews out false accusations, in the manner of weavers and old wives. Peter the Apostle has taught us that the clergy should not be lords over God's heritage but rather examples to their flock, and St. Paul wrote to the Galatians: "My little children, bearing you I travail in birth again until Christ be formed in you." Let our Lord Paschal pay attention to such pious admonitions, rather than to false calumnies. Our Lord Paschal reproaches us and declares us excommunicate, but we will pay more attention to what the Holy Spirit said through the mouth of the Psalmist: "Cursed be they who disobey Thy commands." We utterly reject the curse of excommunication, which, wholly departing from tradition, Hildebrand (Gregory VII), Odo (Urban II), and now this third prelate (Paschal II) have so thoughtlessly levied against us. Rather we venerate and follow the holy fathers who have preceded these popes, who speaking with the Holy Spirit and not with disturbed emotions, have dealt with faults moderately, passing over some,

SOURCE. Mansi, *Sacrorum Conciliorum Nova et Amplissimo Collectio*, XX, pp. 987–999. Translated for this volume by Jeffrey B. Russell.

correcting some, and tolerating others. Our Lord the Bishop is accustomed to close relations with his king and emperor, to whom he has sworn his faith. A great deal of time has gone by since this custom began, and many holy and revered bishops have followed this custom even unto the day of their death, rendering unto Caesar the things that are Caesar's and unto God the things that are God's.

[Now follows a section of citations from St. Ambrose and St. Augustine to the effect that kings have proper authority, and if one does not wish to be under the jurisdiction of kings one ought to give away one's possessions entirely.]

Therefore, following the words of these and other holy fathers, our bishops have taken care to be obedient to their kings and emperors, submitting to their royal authority, lest bishops slay kings with their own sword, that is, with their benefices. Briefly, if anyone with respect for the guidance of the Holy Spirit thinks about the Old and New Testaments and about Christian history it will be obvious to him that kings and emperors can be excommunicated only with difficulty and hardly at all. This is according to the etymology of their names and according to the definition of excommunication. Anyway, up until now, such disputes have been under God. No doubt kings can be admonished, rebuked, and denounced by cautious and discreet men, for those whom Christ has established on Earth as his vicegerents he has left under his judgment. Look here, why are we declared excommunicate, simply because we are holding to the teachings of holy, moderate, and ancient Fathers of the Church? We ought not to be condemned but to be imitated. We obey our bishop, our archbishop, and our provincial synod, in obedience to ancient tradition, and whatever is decided by those authorities in accordance with the teaching of the Holy Scripture ought not to be referred to Rome by those whose authority is nowhere found in the Holy Scripture. I mean those legates *a latere* who run out from the Roman Bishop and hop back into his pouch. We reject these legates completely. . . . Because we hold to the ancient customs of the Church and because we are not blown hither and yon by every breath of new doctrine, those are the reasons for which we have been called excommunicate. . . . Why does Lord Paschal want us to do penance for sins we have not committed? Why does he want us to be called false clerics when we have held to the right path? Let him rather put aside the spirit of false pride and with his counsellors remember carefully how popes used to come into power from the time of Sylvester I up until the time of Hildebrand. Let him remember how many and how great were the marvelous things accomplished by the Holy See and how these things were carried out by kings and emperors and how false popes have been condemned and forced to abdicate. In all this the imperial power has been worth a great deal more than excommunications proclaimed by Hildebrand (Gregory VII), Odo (Urban II), or Paschal.... Pope Hildebrand, who was the originator of this new schism, and who was the first to set the lance of the priesthood against the crown of the king, began by groundlessly excommunicating all the followers of King Henry [and calling] Henry the chief of all the heretics.

[Elsewhere Sigebert accuses the reform papacy of encouraging heresy by its attack upon simony, clerical marriage, and lay investiture.]

8   *The Pataria*

The closeness of heretical and orthodox reform appears in the eleventh-century Florentine movement called the Pataria, long supported by the papacy but charged by its enemies with heresy.

The Pataria was condemned as heretical by its opponents. A Milanese chronicler (Landulfus Senior) maintained that its adherents were followers of the heretics of Monteforte, who were as inimical to the priesthood as to marriage. Others claimed that the Patarini condemned, not only the simoniacs, but also the eucharist, and that they defiled the host and the oil and water of baptism. Yet in fact the Patarini never heretically attacked the doctrine and practices of the Church or the clergy as a whole, but limited their criticism to "unworthy priests:" those who practiced simony or who kept women and whose orders they therefore considered illegitimate. The movement arose in 1057 when Ariald, a deacon who had been educated abroad, began to preach passionately against the immorality of his clerical colleagues. Erlembald, a knight, and his brother Rudolf, became the leaders of the movement. These reform-minded men readily found

SOURCE. Herbert Grundmann, *Ketzergeschichte des Mittelalters* (Göttingen: Vandenhoeck & Ruprecht, 1963), pp. G14–G15. Translated for this volume by Jeffrey B. Russell. Reprinted by permission of the publisher.

acceptance and followers, particularly among the poorer people of the Lombard cities, and the whole movement was labeled by its opponents "Pataria" after the Milanese "flea market."[1] However, although the Patarini directed their strongest attacks against the nobly born cathedral clergy, who lived exactly like their lay cousins, refusing to practice celibacy or to give up their rights and privileges either in the Church or in the world at large, and although social considerations were certainly important in the movement, the essence of the Pataria was neither social nor political, but religious and ecclesiastical; it aimed not at a revolutionary change in social or class conditions but at the purification of the Church. To this end poor laymen arose and sought power, swearing as in a holy war to struggle against the simoniacs and refusing to recognize their orders or their sacraments. The reform movement then indeed became a revolution against the heretofore unassailable domination of the Church by the nobility. Many reform-oriented contemporaries of the Pataria, like Saint Peter Damian, who in 1059 came to Milan as cardinal-legate in order to calm matters down, wondered whether the uproar of the laity against the simoniacs was going to be transformed into a general opposition against the hierarchy in which the efficacy of the sacraments would be deemed dependent upon the worthiness of the priests. But both Gregory VII and the predecessor whose adviser he had been, Alexander II, made use of the movement in order to advance the authority of the pope against the claims of the archbishopric of Milan and in order to combat the claim of the emperor to the right of bestowing investiture upon the archbishop. In 1064, Erlembald, the warlike leader of the Pataria, received a banner blessed by the pope as a mark of Rome's support, and when he died in a street fight in Milan in 1075, Gregory VII permitted his followers to venerate him as a martyr. Nonetheless, when Rome had obtained the goals sought by its own reform policy at Milan, the curia lost interest in the Pataria. By the next century the term "Patarini" had become a synonym for "heretics," particularly for the Italian Catharists. Whether—or how—these revolutionary stormtroopers of Papal Reform actually continued to influence heretical movements is impossible to determine clearly.

---

[1] The origin of the name is still disputed. By another etymology the Patarini are the "ragged ones."—Ed.

9   *Valdes*

Valdes is the perfect type of the Reformist heretic. Wishing only to reform the Church, never to challenge it, he and his followers were driven into heresy by the indifference or hostility of the ecclesiastical authorities. Between Valdes of Lyon the heretic and Francis of Assisi the saint there was little difference save that Francis appeared at a time when the papacy was more willing to accommodate the spirit of enthusiasm.

a. *The following is a general account of the Valdesians (Waldensians) taken from Raymonde Foreville and Jean Rousset de Pina*, Du premier concile du Latran à l'avènement d'Innocent III.

Between 1170 and 1180, a rich merchant of Lyon, Peter,[1] with the surname of Valdo or Valdes, had gathered together several disciples and begun to preach the Gospel. Then he had gone on to distribute his goods to the poor, in order to put into practice the advice of the Gospels. By his example he encouraged men and women to follow him in devoting themselves to absolute poverty and to preaching based on translations of the Bible into the vernacular, in spite of the fact that the authorities of the Church had expressly forbidden laymen to preach. Pope Alexander III—whom Valdes had apparently asked for permission to preach at the time of the Lateran Council of 1179—and also the Archbishop of Lyon, Jean Bellesmains, who, having become archbishop in 1182, did not delay in banning the followers of Valdes from his diocese. In 1184, Lucius III formally condemned the sect at the Council of Verona.

At that time the Valdesians had already spread into the Dauphiné, into Provence, into Piedmont, and into Lombardy where they gave their support to the Humiliati and to the Arnoldists. However in spite of their penetration into Languedoc, and even into Germany, the valleys of the Dauphiné and of Piedmont remained their particular stronghold, and it is difficult to say whether their name derives from the personal name of Valdes or whether Valdes himself took

SOURCE. Raymonde Foreville and Jean Rousset de Pina, *Du premier concile du Latran à l'avènement d'Innocent III* (Paris: Librairie Bloud & Gay, 1953), pp. 342–343. Translated for this volume by Jeffrey B. Russell. Reprinted by permission of the publisher.

[1] Actually, there is no reliable evidence for the traditional name Peter—Ed.

his surname from the fact that his disciples dwelt in the valleys.

The Valdesians repudiated manual labor, lived by begging, and advocated celibacy and the separation of husband and wife. They believed in the divinity of Christ, in man's sinfulness, and in salvation by Jesus Christ. They retained the sacraments of Penance and of the eucharist, but they denied transubstantiation and the Communion of Saints, and they believed that every just man had the power of preaching the Gospel, absolving from sin, and of presiding over the Lord's Supper. Very early they organized themselves into an institutional sect, with a hierarchy and an initiation ceremony somewhat similar to those of the Catharists. They held to the Bible as their supreme authority, and they spread abroad translations that they had hastily made from the New Testament and the Prophets into the vernacular.

If certain similarities of doctrine or practice sometimes caused confusion between the Valdesians and the Catharists, particularly in Languedoc, it was even easier to confuse the Valdesians with the Humiliati, who very early came into contact with the followers of Valdes. There were even some attempts to amalgamate the two heretical groups, who went under the names respectively of The Poor Men of Lombardy and The Poor Men of Lyon. However, the Humiliati did not share the veneration of the Valdesians for Valdes, and, thanks to the efforts of Innocent III, important segments of the Humiliati were received back into the Catholic Church, where they were allowed to remain as religious communities, called the *humiles* and the *Poor Catholics*. On the other hand some remained intractable. As for the Valdesians, their doctrines were solidly planted in the valleys of Lombardy and Switzerland, and in spite of the persecutions that they were forced to undergo, they were still flourishing at the time of the Reformation. They may thus be seen as the distant precursors of the Reformation, which in part absorbed them.

b. *The following is an extract from Bernard Gui's* Manuel de l'Inquisiteur, *ed. G. Mollat*, in a translation by Mary Martin McLaughlin in: James Bruce Ross and Mary Martin McLaughlin,* The Portable Medieval Reader.

The sect and heresy of the Waldensians began in about the year 1170

---

*SOURCE. Bernard Gui, *Manuel de l'Inquisiteur*, G. Mollat, ed. (Paris: Champion, 1926), trans. by Mary Martin McLaughlin, in James Bruce Ross and Mary Martin McLaughlin, *The Portable Medieval Reader* (New York: The Viking Press, Inc., 1949), pp. 202–216. Reprinted by permission of the publisher.

A.D. Its founder was a certain citizen of Lyons, named Waldes or Waldo, from whom his followers were named. He was a rich man, who, after having given up all his wealth, determined to observe poverty and evangelical perfection, in imitation of the apostles. He caused to be translated into the French tongue, for his use, the Gospels, and some other books of the Bible, and also some authoritative sayings of Saints Augustine, Jerome, Ambrose, and Gregory, arranged under titles, which he and his followers called "sentences." They read these very often, and hardly understood them, since they were quite unlettered, but infatuated with their own interpretation, they usurped the office of the apostles, and presumed to preach the Gospel in the streets and public places. And the said Waldes or Waldo converted many people, both men and women, to a like presumption, and sent them out to preach as his disciples.

Since these people were ignorant and illiterate, they, both men and women, ran about through the towns, and entered the houses. Preaching in public places and also in the churches, they, especially the men, spread many errors around about them.

They were summoned, however, by the archbishop of Lyons, the Lord Jean aux Belles-Mains, and were forbidden such great presumption, but they wished by no means to obey him, and cloaked their madness by saying that it was necessary to obey God rather than man. They said that God had commanded the apostles to preach the Gospel to all men, applying to themselves what was said to the apostles whose imitators and successors they boldly declared themselves to be, by a false profession of poverty and the feigned image of sanctity. They scorned the prelates and the clergy, because they abounded in riches and lived in pleasantness.

So then, by this arrogant usurpation of the office of preaching, they became masters of error. Admonished to cease, they disobeyed and were declared contumacious, and then were excommunicated and expelled from that city and their country. Finally in a certain council which was held at Rome before the Lateran council, since they were obstinate, they were judged schismatic, and then condemned as heretics. Thus, multiplied upon the earth, they dispersed themselves through that province, and through the neighbouring regions, and into Lombardy. Separated and cut off from the Church, mingling with other heretics and imbibing their errors, they mixed the errors and heresies of earlier heretics with their own inventions. . . .

CONCERNING THE ERRORS OF THE WALDENSIANS OF MODERN TIMES (SINCE FORMERLY THEY HAD MANY OTHERS)

The principal heresy, then, of the aforesaid Waldensians was and still remains the contempt for ecclesiastical power. Excommunicated for this reason, and delivered to Satan, they were precipitated into innumerable errors, and mingled the errors of earlier heretics with their own.

The erring followers and sacrilegious masters of this sect hold and teach that they are not subject to the lord pope or Roman pontiff or to any prelates of the Roman Church, declaring that the Roman Church has persecuted and condemned them unjustly and undeservedly. Also they assert that they cannot be excommunicated by the Roman pontiff and the prelates, and that they ought not to obey any of them, when they order or command the followers and teachers of the said sect to abandon or abjure it, although this sect has been condemned as heretical by the Roman Church.

Also, they hold and teach that all oaths, whether in justice or otherwise, without exception and explanation, are forbidden by God, and illicit and sinful, interpreting thus in an excessive and unreasonable sense the words of the holy Gospel and of St. James the Apostle against swearing. Nevertheless, the swearing of oaths is lawful and obligatory for the purpose of declaring the truth in justice, according not only to the same doctrine of the saints and doctors of the Church and the tradition of the same holy Catholic Church, but also to the decree of the Church published against the aforesaid error: "If any of these should reject the religious obligation of taking an oath by a damnable superstition, and should refuse to swear, from this fact they may be considered heretics."

It should be known, however, that these Waldensians give themselves dispensations in the matter of taking oaths; they have the right to swear an oath to avoid death for themselves or for another, and also in order not to betray their fellows, or reveal the secret of their sect. For they say that it is an inexpiable crime and a sin against the Holy Ghost to betray a "perfect" member of their sect.

Also, from this same fount of error, the said sect and heresy declares that all judgment is forbidden by God, and consequently is sinful, and that any judge violates this prohibition of God, who in whatever case and for whatever cause sentences a man to corporal punishment, or to a penalty of blood, or to death. In this, they apply, without the necessary explanation, the words of the holy Gospel where it is written: "Judge not, that ye be not judged," and "Thou shalt not kill," and other similar texts; they do not understand these or know either their meaning or their interpretation, as the holy Roman Church wisely understands them and transmits them to the faithful according to the doctrines of the fathers and doctors, and the decisions of canon law.

Also, the aforesaid sect, wandering from the straight and narrow path, does not accept or consider valid the canonical sanctions and the decretals and constitutions of the supreme pontiffs, and the regulations concerning fasts and the celebration of feast days, and the decrees of the fathers, but scorns, rejects, and condemns them.

Also, more perniciously in error concerning the sacrament of penance and the power of keys, the aforesaid heretics say, hold, and teach that they have power from God alone and from no other, just as the apostles had from Christ, of hearing the confessions of the men and women who wish to confess to them and be absolved and have penances imposed on them. And they hear the confessions of such people and absolve them and impose penances, although they are not priests or clerics ordained by any bishop of the Roman Church, but are simply laymen. They do not confess that they hold such power from the Roman Church, but rather deny it, and in fact they hold it neither from God nor from His Church, since they are outside the Church, and are now cut off from that Church outside which there is no true penitence or salvation.

Also, the aforesaid sect and heresy ridicule the indulgences which are made and given by the prelates of the Church and declare that they are worthless.

They are in error indeed concerning the sacrament of the Eucharist, saying, not publicly but secretly, that in the sacrament of the altar the bread and wine do not become the body and blood of Christ if the priest who celebrates or consecrates is a sinner; and they consider any man a sinner who does not belong to their sect. Also, they say that the consecration of the body and blood of Christ may be made by any just person, although he be a layman and not a priest ordained by a Catholic bishop, provided he is a member of their sect. They even believe the same thing concerning women, if they are of their sect, and so they say that every holy person is a priest. . . .

Also, they declare that there are three ranks in their church; deacons, priests, and bishops, and that the power of each of these comes from them only, and not from the Roman Church. They believe that the holy orders of the Roman Church are not from God, but from human tradition and so they falsely deceive when they profess that they believe that there are in the holy church (meaning their own) the holy orders of the episcopate, the priesthood, and the diaconate. . . .

These three doctrines, however, they do not make known indifferently to their "believers," but the "perfect" of this sect hold them among themselves; namely, that the miracles of the saints are not true, that prayers should not be made to them, and that their feasts should not be celebrated, except Sunday, the feasts of the Blessed Virgin Mary, and, some add, the feasts of the apostles and evangelists.

They teach these and other insane and erroneous doctrines, which follow by necessity from those which precede them, secretly to their "believers" in their conventicles. They also preach to them on the Gospels and Epistles and other sacred writings, which these masters of error, who do not know how to be the disciples of truth, distort by their interpretation. For preaching is absolutely forbidden to laymen. It should be known, also, that this sect formerly had and held many other errors, and still in certain regions is said to hold them secretly, such as those concerning the celebration of the mass on Holy Thursday, described above, and the abominable and promiscuous coupling of men and women, under cover of darkness, and concerning the apparition of cats, sprinkling with the tail, and certain others described more fully in the little summaries written on this subject.

CONCERNING THE MANNER OF LIFE OF THE WALDENSIANS

Something should be said concerning the practices and way of life of the Waldensian heretics, in order that they may be known and recognized.

In the first place, then, it should be known that the Waldensians have and establish for themselves one superior whom they call their "majoral" and whom all must obey, just as all Catholics obey the lord pope.

Also, the Waldensians eat and drink at common meals. Also those who can and will, fast on Mondays and Wednesdays; those who fast, however, eat meat. Also, they fast on Fridays, and during Lent, and then they abstain from meat in order not to give scandal to others, since they say that to eat meat on any day whatsoever is not a sin, because Christ did not prohibit the eating of meat, nor order anyone to abstain from it.

Also, after they have been received into this society, which they call a "fraternity," and have promised obedience to their superior, and that they will observe evangelical poverty, from that time they should observe chastity and should not own property, but should sell all that they possess and give the price to the common fund, and live on alms which are given to them by their "believers" and those who sympathize with them. And the superior distributes these among them, and gives to each one according to his needs.

Also, the Waldensians recommend continence to their believers. They concede, however, that burning passion ought to be satisfied, in whatever shameful way, interpreting the words of the Apostle [Paul]: "It is better to marry than to burn," to mean that it is better to appease desire by any shameful act than to be tempted inwardly in the heart. This doctrine they keep very secret, however, in order not to seem vile to their "believers."

Also, they have collections made by their "believers" and friends, and what is given and received they take to their superior.

Also, each year they hold or celebrate one or two general chapters in some important town, as secretly as possible, assembling, as if they were merchants, in a house hired long before by one or more of the "believers." And in those chapters the superior of all orders and disposes matters concerning the priests and deacons and concerning those sent to different parts and regions to their "believers" and friends to hear confessions and to collect alms. He also receives the account of receipts and expenses.

Also, they do not work with their hands after they have been made "perfect," nor do they do any work for profit, except perchance in case it is necessary to dissimulate, so that they may not be recognized and apprehended.

Also, they commonly call themselves brothers, and they say that they are the poor of Christ or the poor of Lyons.

Also, they hypocritically insinuate themselves into the society of the religious and of the clergy, so that they may conceal themselves, and they bestow gifts or presents upon them and pay them reverence and services so that they may obtain a freer opportunity for themselves and theirs to hide, to live, and to injure souls.

Also, they frequent the churches and sermons, and in all externals conduct themselves with religion and compunction, and strive to use unctuous and discreet language.

Also, they say many prayers during the day, and they instruct their "believers" that they should pray as they do, and with them. This is their manner of praying: on bended knees, they bow down on a bench or on something like it, and so, on their knees, bowed down to the ground, they all remain praying in silence for as long as it takes to say the "Our Father" thirty or forty times or more. They do this regularly each day, when they are with their "believers" and sympathizers, with no strangers present, before and after dinner, before and after supper, at night when they go to bed, before they lie down; also in the morning when they arise, and in the course of the day, both in the morning and in the afternoon.

Also, they say and teach and recognize no other prayer besides the "Our Father." They have no regard for the salutation of the Virgin Mary, "Hail, Mary," or for the Apostles' Creed, "I believe in God," for they say that these have been arranged or composed by the Roman Church and not by Christ. They keep, however, seven articles of the faith on divinity, seven on humanity, and the ten commandments of the Decalogue, and the seven works of mercy. They have arranged and composed these in a sort of résumé and in a certain way, and they say and teach them thus. They glory exceedingly in this and they show themselves immediately ready to answer concerning their faith.

They can thus easily be detected in this way: "Say for me the Apostles' Creed, as the Catholic Church says it, since it contains all the articles" and then they answer: "I do not know it, because no one has taught me thus." . . .

Also, they tell their "believers" that they should in no way betray them to chaplains or clerics or religious or inquisitors, because, if they should be known, they would be seized. They are pursued by the inquisitors and those of the Roman Church unjustly, they say to their "believers," because it is they who serve God and observe the commandments of God and practise poverty and evangelical perfection, just as Christ and the apostles did. They say that they themselves know the truth and the way of God better than the chaplains and clerics and religious of the Roman Church, who persecuted them through ignorance of the truth. . . .

ON THE METHOD OF TEACHING OF THE WALDENSIANS

One can distinguish two categories in this sect; there are the "perfect," and these are properly called Waldensians. These, previously instructed, are received into their order according to a special rite, so that they may know how to teach others. These "perfect" claim that they possess nothing of their own, neither houses nor possessions nor furnishings. Moreover, if they had had wives before, they give them up when they are received. They say that they are the successors of the apostles, and are the masters and confessors of the others. They travel through the country, visiting and confirming their disciples in error. Their disciples and "believers" supply them with necessities. Wherever the "perfect" go, the "believers" spread the news of their arrival, and many come to the house, where they are admitted to see and hear them. All sorts of good things to eat and drink are brought to them, and their preaching is heard in assemblies which gather chiefly at night, when others are sleeping or resting.

The "perfect," moreover, do not immediately in the beginning reveal the secrets of their error. First they say what the disciples of Christ should be like, according to the words of the Gospel and of the apostles. Only those, they say, should be the successors of the apostles who imitate and hold to the example of their life. On this basis, they argue and conclude that the pope, the bishops and prelates, and clergy, who possess the riches of this world and do not imitate the sanctity of the apostles, are not true pastors and guides of the Church of God, but ravening and devouring wolves, to whom Christ did not deign to entrust His spouse the Church, and so they should not be obeyed. They also say that an impure person cannot purify another, nor can one who is bound loose another, nor can an accused person influence a judge, already angered against him, in favour of another accused person. One who is on the road to perdition cannot lead another to heaven. In this way, they slander the clergy and the prelates, in order to render them odious, so that they will not be believed or obeyed.

The Waldensians, then, commonly say and teach to their "believers" certain things which seem good and moral, concerning the virtues which should be practised, the good works which should be done, and the vices to be avoided and fled from. Thus they are more readily listened to in other matters, and they ensnare their hearers. For they say that one should not lie, since everyone who lies slays his soul, according to the Scripture; also that one should not do to another, what he would not want done to him. One should obey the commandments of God. One should not swear in any case because God has forbidden all taking of oaths, saying in the Gospel: "Swear not at all; neither by heaven; for it is God's throne: Nor by the earth for it is the footstool of His feet, nor by any other creature, because a man cannot make one hair white or black, but let your speaking be yea, yea, and nay, nay; for whatever is more than these comes of evil." These words make a great impression on their "believers" and they receive no further interpretation of them. . . .

Also, when they preach on the Gospels and the Epistles, or on the examples or sayings of the saints, they allege: "This is written in the Gospel or in the Epistle of St. Peter or St. Paul or St. James, or the writings of such and such a saint or doctor," so that what they say may be more readily accepted by their hearers.

Moreover, they ordinarily have the Gospels and the Epistles in the vulgar tongue, and also in Latin, since some of them understand it. Some also know how to read, and sometimes they read from a book those things which they say and preach. Sometimes they do not use a book, especially those who do not read, but they have learned these things by heart. . . .

Also, they teach their "believers" that true penitence and the purgatory of sins are only in this life and not in another. And so they instruct their "believers" to confess their sins to them, and they hear confessions, and absolve those who confess to them, and impose penances on them, consisting usually of fasting on Friday and of saying the "Our Father." They say that they have this power from God, just as the apostles had.

Also, according to them, when souls leave their bodies, those which should be saved go immediately to heaven, and those which should be damned immediately to hell. There is no other place for souls, after this life, except paradise or hell.

Also they say that the prayers which are said for the dead are of no avail for them, because those who are in paradise do not need them and for those who are in hell there is no redemption.

Also, when they hear confessions, they tell those who are confessing that they should not reveal, when they confess to priests, that they have made confessions to those Waldensians.

CONCERNING THE SUBTLETIES AND DECEITS WITH WHICH THEY CONCEAL THEMSELVES IN ANSWERING

It should be known that it is exceedingly difficult to interrogate and examine the Waldensians, and to get the truth about their errors from them, because of the deception and duplicity with which they answer questions, in order not to be caught. . . .

This is the way they do it. When one of them is arrested and brought for examination, he appears undaunted, and as if he were secure and conscious of no evil in himself. When he is asked if he knows why he has been arrested, he answers very sweetly and with a smile, "My Lord, I should be glad to learn the reason from you." Asked about the faith which he holds and believes, he answers, "I believe everything that a good Christian ought to believe." Questioned as to whom he considers a good Christian, he replies, "He who believes as Holy Church teaches him to believe." When he is asked what he means by "Holy Church," he answers, "My lord, that which you say and believe is the Holy Church." If you say to him, "I believe that the Holy Church is the Roman Church, over which the lord pope rules, and under him, the prelates," he replies, "I believe it," meaning that he believes that you believe it.

Interrogated concerning the articles in which he believes, such as the Incarnation of Christ, His Resurrection and Ascension, he promptly answers, "I firmly believe." Asked if he believes that in the mass the bread and wine are transubstantiated into the body and blood of Christ by the words of the priest and by the divine power, he says, "Should I not, indeed, believe this?" If the inquisitor says, "I do not ask if you should believe, but if you do not believe," he replies, "I believe whatever you and other good doctors command me to believe." . . .

When he is questioned concerning this deception and many others like it, and asked to answer explicitly and directly, he replies, "If you will not interpret what I say simply and sanely, then I do not know how I should answer you. I am a simple and illiterate man. Do not try to ensnare me in my words." If you say to him, "If you are a simple man, answer simply, without dissimulation," he says, "Willingly."

Then if you say, "Will you swear that you have never learned anything contrary to the faith which we say and believe to be true," he answers somewhat timorously, "If I ought to swear, I shall willingly swear." "I am not asking whether you ought to swear, but whether you will swear." Then he replies, "If you command me to swear, I shall swear." I say to him, "I do not compel you to swear, because, since you believe that it is forbidden to take an oath, you will put the blame on me for compelling you; but if you want to swear, I shall listen." Then he answers, "Why should I swear then, if you will not command me?" "To remove the suspicion that you are reputed to be a Waldensian heretic who believes that all swearing of oaths is unlawful and sinful." He then replies, "How ought I to swear?" You say, "Swear as you know." He answers, "My lord, I do not know, unless you teach me." "If I should have to swear, then with hand upraised, and touching the holy Gospels of God, I should say, 'I swear by these holy Gospels that I have never learned or believed anything contrary to the faith which the holy Roman Church believes and holds.'" Then, trembling and as if he did not know how to form the words, he stammers over them, he stops, as if interrupted, and he puts in words, to avoid the direct formula of the oath, but uses certain expressions, which are not swearing, so that he will seem to have sworn. . . .

If, however, one of these heretics consents to swear simply, then you should say to him, "If you now swear in order to be released, you should know that one oath or two or ten or a hundred are not enough for me, but as many as I shall ask. For I know that you are dispensed, and are permitted a certain number of oaths when compelled by necessity, so that you may free yourself or others. But I mean to require of you oaths without number and, moreover, if I have witnesses against you, your oaths will profit you nothing. And then you have stained your conscience by swearing contrary to its dictates and because of this you will not escape."

I have seen some of them who, in such great anxiety, confessed their errors, in order to escape. Others, however, then declared openly that, if it would be of no avail for their escape to swear once or a certain number of times and no more, they refused to swear at all, and said that all swearing is unlawful and sinful. And when one of them was asked why he wished to swear, if he considered it unlawful, he replied: "I wish to deliver myself from death by doing this, and to conserve my life, and I shall do penance afterward for my sin."

c. *The following is from a book by Alan of Lille entitled* On the Catholic Faith Against the Heretics of his Time. *This book was written in 1200–1202, and the second part is entitled* Against the Waldensians. *I follow the edition of Giovanni Gonnet,* Enchiridion Fontium Valdensium. *I give the whole of the first section and then merely the chapter headings, which indicate the doctrines of the Valdesians according to Alan of Lille.*

Chapter I: *By what authority and for what reason it is shown that no one ought to preach unless he has permission from the bishop.* There are certain heretics who claim to be just, when they are really wolves in sheep's

SOURCE. Alan of Lille, *Against the Waldensians* (1200–1202), in Giovanni Gonnet, *Enchiridion Fontium Valdensium* (Torre Pellice, 1958), pp. 103–119. Translated for this volume by Jeffrey B. Russell.

clothing, for within they are ravening wolves. These heretics are called Waldenses, after their heresiarch, who was named Waldus, who —led by his emotions, not sent by God—founded a new sect and presumed to preach without the authority of the Bishop, without divine inspiration, without knowledge, and without literacy. He was an irrational philosopher, a prophet without vision, an apostle without a mission, a teacher without an instructor, and his foolish disciples have led the simple folk astray in many parts of the world. They have turned them away from the truth rather than turning them toward the truth. They presume to preach, though they are more capable of filling the belly than the mind, and since they do not want to work with their hands in order to acquire their food, they prefer to live slothful lives and to earn their food by false preaching. . . .

Chapter II: By what authority and to what end the Waldenses say that no one ought to be obedient to anyone except to God.

Chapter V: The opinion of those who say that it is necessary to be obedient only to good bishops.

Chapter VIII: The opinion of those who say that priestly office or ordination does not confer the right to consecrate or to bless, to bind or to loose.

Chapter IX: The opinion of those who say that general absolutions given by bishops are not valid.

Chapter XII: The opinion of those who say that prayers offered up by people in mortal sin are of no use to the dead.[2]

Chapter XV: The opinion of those who say that every lie is a mortal sin.

Chapter XVIII: The opinion of those who say that on no account must one swear an oath.

Chapter XX: The opinion of those who say that there is no legitimate reason for killing a man.

Chapter XXIV: The opinion of those who say that preachers ought not work with their hands.

---

[2] This refers to the belief of the Valdesians that prayers and sacraments offered by sinful priests were not valid.—Ed.

PART III

Radical Revolution: the Catharists

Catharism probably appeared in Western Europe in the 1140s, strongly influenced by Bogomilism. The Bogomils, like the Patarenes of Illyria,[1] were dualists whose ideas were ultimately derived from the ancient gnostics and Manichaeans of the Middle East. Because of tendencies toward ascetic, otherworldly, dualist thought in Christianity itself, and particularly among the Reformist heretics, Catharism spread rapidly and widely, with its centers in southern France and northern Italy. Reformism paved the way for Catharism, and it was precisely in those areas where Reformism had been strong that Catharism now flourished. The most dramatic example of the capture of a Reformist group by Catharism is provided by the events at Cologne from 1145 to 1163. In 1145 there was a sect of Reformists in that city; later there were two groups of heretics at odds; and finally a Catharist group with a minority apparently still adhering to the old, Reformist positions.

The Catharists believed that there were two powerful and antagonistic spiritual forces in the universe. The earlier Catharists tended to be "mitigated dualists," believing that the evil force was a creature inferior to God. Later Catharists tended to be absolute dualists, positing two equal and coeternal deities. The elite of their sect, the *perfecti* ("perfect ones") had taken the *consolamentum* or initiatory sacrament and practised an extreme asceticism worthy of their beliefs; but the *credentes* or simple "believers" were evidently allowed to be very loose in their morals with the excuse that when they later took the *consolamentum* it would purify them of their sins. The doctrines and practices of the Catharists offended the orthodox equally; St.

[1] Not the Italian Patarini.

55

Bernard, St. Dominic, and many other preachers attempted to convert the heretics to Catholicism, but their strength only grew. In southern France, a large proportion of the population of all social classes by the beginning of the thirteenth century subscribed to Catharism, and the spiritual power of the sect was supplemented by the temporal support of such rulers as Count Raymond VI of Toulouse. The influence of the Catharists was finally dissipated by the bloody Albigensian Crusade, preached by Innocent III and implemented by King Louis VII of France, Simon de Montfort, and other northern French leaders who wished to enrich themselves at the expense of the southerners.

10   *Summary of Catharist Beliefs*

The following is a summary of typical Catharist beliefs of the thirteenth century. Some of the variations of the type will be seen in subsequent selections. This summary is taken from Jeffrey B. Russell, Dissent and Reform in the Early Middle Ages.

The fundamental supposition of the true dualists was that there are two opposing forces in the world, one good and one evil. Whether or not the power of evil was independent of the good God or one of his fallen angels was debated, but in either event it was he, rather than the good God, who created the world. The phenomenal world, having entrapped spirit in matter, was evil. The God of the Old Testament created the world and was the evil god. The Old Testament was therefore to be rejected, exception being sometimes made for the books of the prophets, who were believed to have predicted the coming of Christ. Man was in a difficult position: his soul was spiritual and therefore good; he must seek to liberate it from the flesh as effectively as he could. By living the proper life (that is, by becoming a Catharist), one could escape the flesh; otherwise the spirit might be doomed to reincarnation. Purgatory was rejected in favor of metempsychosis, as was the resurrection of the dead. Water being corrupt and therefore impotent for good, baptism in the ordinary Christian sense was rejected. The baptism of infants was frowned upon in particular, for children were creatures in which spirit had been newly entrapped. No one could be saved until he had reached the age when initiation into the Catharist religion was permitted. Christ could not have had a true human body since the divine would not have clothed itself in a garment of evil flesh. His suffering on the cross was therefore an illusion, as was his resurrection. The Virgin Mary was often given little respect, for her fleshly body could not really have given birth to God. At most she was designated as an angel along with her son. Then, Jesus being an angel rather than very God, the doctrine of the Trinity was denied. Jesus' mission was not to redeem us through his passion,

SOURCE. Jeffrey B. Russell, *Dissent and Reform in the Early Middle Ages* (Berkeley and Los Angeles, University of California Press, 1965), pp. 202–205. Reprinted by permission of the publisher.

but rather to convey to us prisoners of the flesh instructions for effecting an escape from the body. Since Christ's body was an illusion
and the eucharist matter, that sacrament was a delusion. The cross
and all images were matter and therefore contemptible. The cult of the
saints was rejected, as was the Christian sacrament of penance.

With all this, it was natural that the dualist denied the authority
of the Catholic Church, which was an institution of the evil god designed to keep men enslaved to matter. In place of the Catholic hierarchy, the Catharists had bishops of their own, but no pope. Local
Catharists were organized into groups in which a division was sharply
drawn between the *perfecti* on the one hand and the *credentes* on the
other. Admission to the sect was obtained through the rite known as
the *convenientia*. This made one a *credens* and put one under the authority
of the *perfecti*. In certain instances, particularly when they were suspected of having had doubts as to their belief, the *credentes* were
obliged to adore the *perfecti*. After long instruction and practice in
mortifying the flesh, including a year of exceptionally rigorous abstinence, the *consolamentum* was administered, and the *credens* became
a *perfectus*. The rigors of this period were so great that it sometimes
ended in death, which, if it occurred after the administration of the
consolamentum, the great sacrament of the Catharists, was not to be
regretted, since it meant the final liberation of soul from body. Later,
and in certain areas, the *endura*, or fasting unto death, was occasionally
administered, especially to children or to the sick, with the express
purpose of effecting such a liberation. In these instances the *consolamentum* was administered at the end of the ordeal; then, if one survived, he became a *perfectus*. He was then a full initiate of the sect,
wore special black clothing, and was expected to lead a life of utter
purity, since the *consolamentum*, which filled the part of Catholic
baptism, confirmation, extreme unction, and, in a way, holy orders as
well, could not be repeated. This sacrament was bestowed by the lay-
ing-on of hands, the *perfecti* initiating a believer in a rite similar to
the consecration of Catholic bishops.

The Catharists had other customs of a semisacramental nature.
They had three long fasts annually. They performed public penance
for public sin, private penance for private sin. Once a month they held
a *servitium*, a service at which confessions of petty sins (the *perfecti*
had no serious sins) were made and penances assigned. A resemblance
to early Christianity is discernible, when sin after baptism was often
considered unforgivable and many people for this reason put off the
reception of the sacrament until late in life. An elaborate ritual feast

was celebrated. The kiss of peace, a double kiss, was common between *perfecti*. The *melioramentum*, a special form of greeting between members of the sect, was also employed, usually between a *credens* and a *perfectus*.

The *perfecti* lived lives of ascetic rigor. They forbade the use of oaths. They rejected luxury and wealth (at least in theory; the nobles and bourgeois of Provence did not often abandon castle and house). They abstained from meat, partly because of their belief in metempsychosis. This same belief prohibited their killing most animals, particularly four-footed animals and birds, though snakes, insects, and other lowly creatures might be killed because they were purely evil and had no spirit within them. Meat was eschewed for the additional reason that it was a food engendered by procreation. The Catharists avoided other foods associated with generation, notably eggs, cheese, and milk. This aversion to procreation, as well as their attitude toward marriage and sex in general, stems from the fact that it is the sexual act that is responsible for imprisoning spirits in the flesh. Marriage was absolutely to be avoided; if it could not be, the spouses were at least to live in celibacy. Among the Catharists, it was less a feeling that sexual pleasure in itself was bad than an aversion to childbearing that determined their attitude. Promiscuity outside marriage was almost as bad as marriage itself, but it was the institutionalized wedded state that was particulary blameworthy. Two exceptions to this rule of sexual abstinence may have existed. Orthodox writers frequently condemned the Catharists for sexual laxity. This is a cliché in orthodox writing about heretics of all varieties: heresy is evil; a heretic is evil; ergo, he does all kinds of evil things. But where there is much smoke there may be some fire. The Catharist aversion to procreation would not have excluded sexual activities that could not result in conception, and the unnatural vices of which they were accused may not have existed entirely in the imaginations of their accusers. Psychoanalysis gives a hint as to the possible motivation of such deviations. Herbert Marcuse says of Orpheus, the founder (at least in myth) of Greek dualism, that, "Like Narcissus, he rejects the normal Eros, not for an ascetic ideal, but for a fuller Eros. Like Narcissus, he protests against the repressive order of procreative sexuality." In addition, it must be remembered that the *credentes* were under no such compulsion to purity as were the *perfecti*, since the *consolamentum* always lay in their future, and they very likely indulged in excesses that their leaders would have eschewed.

11   *The Heretics of Cologne*

The transition from Reformist to Catharist heresy at Cologne in the twelfth century is illustrated by the following documents, translated by Peter Allix and Samuel Roffey Maitland. Between 1143 and 1145 Evervinus, a Premonstratensian prior of Steinfeld, wrote to Saint Bernard of Clairvaux concerning heretics at Cologne. Evervinus distinguished between two groups, the first already strongly influenced by Catharist beliefs; the second still purely Reformist.

---

a. Letter of Evervinus.   There have been lately some heretics discovered amongst us, near Cologne, whereof some with satisfaction returned again to the Church: two of these, viz. one that was a Bishop amongst them, and his companions, openly opposed us in the assembly of the clergy and laity, the Lord Archbishop himself being present, with many of the nobility, maintaining their heresy from the words of Christ and the Apostles. But when they saw they could go no further, they desired that a day might be appointed for them, upon which they might bring along with them men skilful in their belief, promising to return to the church, provided they should find their masters defective in answering what was opposed to them; but that otherwise they would rather die than depart from their judgment. Upon this their declaration, after that for three days together they had been admonished, and found unwilling to repent, they were seized by the people, being incited to overmuch zeal, and put into the fire and burnt; and (what is most wonderful) they entered to the stake, and bare the torment of the fire, not only with patience, but with joy and gladness. In this case, O Holy Father, were I present with you, I should be glad to have your answer, how these members of the Devil could with such courage and constancy persist in their heresy, as is scarcely to be found in the most religious in the faith of Christ.

Their heresy is this: they say that the Church is only amongst them, because they alone follow the steps of Christ, and continue in the imitation of the true apostolic life, not seeking the things of this world, possessing neither house, lands, nor anything in propriety, according as Christ did, who neither possessed any himself, nor gave leave to

SOURCE. Peter Allix and Samuel Roffey Maitland, trans., *Facts and Documents Illustrative of the History, Doctrine, and Rites, of the Ancient Albigenses and Waldenses* (London: Rivington, 1832), pp. 344–350.

his disciples to possess anything. Whereas ye (say they to us) join house
to house, and field to field, seeking the things of this world; so that
even they also, who are looked upon as most perfect amongst you,
such as are your Monks and Regular Canons, though they do not possess these things as proper, but as common, yet do they possess all
these things. And of themselves they say, We the poor of Christ, who
have no certain abode, fleeing from one city to another, like sheep
in the midst of wolves, do endure persecution with the Apostles and
Martyrs: notwithstanding that we lead an holy and strict life in fasting
and abstinence, persevering day and night in prayers and labours, and
seeking only from thence what is necessary to support our lives. We
undergo this, because we are not of the world; but ye lovers of the
world, ye have peace with the world, because ye are of the world.
False Apostles, who adulterate the word of Christ, seeking their own,
have misled you and your forefathers; whereas we and our fathers,
being born Apostles, have continued in the grace of Christ, and shall
continue so to the end of the world. To distinguish between us and
you, Christ saith, "By their fruits ye shall know them": our fruits are
the footsteps of Christ. In their diet they forbid all manner of milk,
and whatsoever is made of it, and all that is procreated by copulation.
This is that which they oppose to us concerning their conversation.
As to the Sacraments, they conceal themselves; yet did they openly
confess to us, that daily at their tables, when they take their meals, they,
according to the form of Christ and his Apostles, do consecrate their
meat and drink into the body and blood of Christ, by the Lord's
Prayer, to nourish themselves therewith, as being the members and
body of Christ. But as for us, they say we hold not the truth in the
Sacraments, but only a kind of shadow, and tradition of men. They
also openly confess, that besides water, they baptized also with fire
and the Holy Ghost, and had been so baptized themselves; alleging to
to this purpose the testimony of St. John the Baptist, baptizing with
water, and saying concerning Christ, "He shall baptize you with the
Holy Ghost and with fire": and in another place, "I indeed baptize
you with water, but there stands one in the midst of you, whom you
know not, who shall baptize you with another baptism besides that of
water." And that this other baptism was to be performed by the im-
position of hands, they endeavoured to make out by the testimony of
St. Luke, who, in the Acts of the Apostles, describing Paul's baptism,
which he received from Ananias, at the command of Christ, makes no
mention of water, but only the laying on of hands; and whatsoever
else we find, whether in the Acts of the Apostles or in St. Paul's Epistles,

they apply to this baptism; and they say that every elect (for so they call all those that are baptized amongst them) hath power to baptize others whom they find worthy, and to consecrate the body and blood of Christ at their meals. For first, by their laying on of hands, they receive some of their auditors into the number of believers, and then they have leave to be present at their prayers, until that, after having had sufficient trial of them, they make them elect. They condemn our baptism, condemn marriage; but the reason why, I could not get out of them, either because they durst not own it, or rather because they knew none.

There are also some other heretics in our country, who are altogether different from these, by whose mutual discord and contests they were both of them discovered to us. These deny that the body of Christ is made on the Altar, because all the Priests of the Church are not consecrated. For the Apostolic dignity (say they) is corrupted, engaging itself in secular affairs; and, in the chair of Peter, not waging God's warfare, like Peter, it has deprived itself of the power of consecrating, which was given to Peter; and what it has not itself, the Archbishops and Bishops, who live like men of the world, cannot receive from it, viz. the power of consecrating others: to this purpose alleging these words of Christ, "The Scribes and Pharisees sit in Moses's chair; what therefore they bid you do, that do." As if such as these had only the power of preaching and commanding, but nothing more. Thus they make void the Priesthood of the Church, and condemn the Sacraments besides Baptism only; and this only in those who are come to age, who, they say, are baptized by Christ himself, whosoever be the Minister of the Sacraments. They do not believe infant baptism citing that place of the Gospel, "Whosoever shall believe, and be baptized, shall be saved." All marriage they call fornication, besides that which is between two virgins, male and female; quoting for this the words of our Saviour, wherewith he answers the Pharisees, "What God hath joined let no man separate"; as if God did only join such together, as he did our first parents: as likewise those words of our Saviour, which he speaks to the Jews, in answer to what they objected to him about the bill of divorce, "From the beginning it was not so"; and the following words, "Whosover marrieth her that is divorced, commits adultery"; and that of the Apostle, "Let marriage be honourable to all, and the bed undefiled."

They put no confidence in the intercession of the Saints; they maintain that fasting, and other afflictions which are undertaken for sin, are not necessary to the just, nor to sinners; because at what time soever the sinner repents of his sin, they are all forgiven to him, and all other things observed in the Church, which have not been established by Christ himself or his Apostles, they call superstitions. They do not admit of any purgatory fire after death; but that the souls, as soon as they depart out of the bodies, do enter into rest or punishment; proving it from that place of Solomon, "Which way soever the tree falls whether to the south or to the north, there it lies": by which means they make void all the prayers and oblations of believers for the deceased.

We therefore desire you Holy Father, to employ your care and watchfulness against these manifold mischiefs, and that you would be pleased to direct your pen against these wild beasts of the reeds; not thinking it sufficient to answer us, that the tower of David, to which we may take our refuge, is sufficiently fortified with bulwarks, that a thousand bucklers hang on the walls of it, all shields of mighty men. For we desire, Father, that for the sake of us simple ones, and that are slow of understanding, you would be pleased by your study to gather all these arms in one place, that they may be the more ready to be found, and more powerful to resist these monsters. I let you know also, that those of them who have returned to our Church, told us that they had great numbers of their persuasion scattered almost every where: and that amongst them were many of our Clergy and Monks. And as for those who were burnt, they, in the defence they made for themselves, told us, that this their heresy, had been concealed from the time of the Martyrs until these times; and that it had been preserved in Greece, and some other countries. These are those heretics who call themselves Apostles, having a Pope of their own; whereas the others despise our Pope, and yet own themselves to have no other besides him. These Apostles of Satan have amongst them continent women, (as they call them) widows, virgins, their wives, some of which are amongst the number of their elect, others of their believers; as in imitation of the Apostles, who had power to lead about women with them. Farewell in the Lord.

b. *Eckbert of Schönau.* In *1163*, *Eckbert, a canon of Bonn and later abbot of Schönau in the diocese of Trier, wrote a book against the Catharists in the region of Cologne. The book, addressed to the archbishop of Cologne, shows that the Catharist elements first visible in the 1140s had twenty years later become firmly entrenched.*

SOURCE. Peter Allix and Samuel Roffey Maitland, trans., *Facts and Documents illustrative of the History, Doctrine, and Rites, of the Ancient Albigenses and Waldenses* (London: Rivington, 1832), pp. 350–362.

It often happens in your [the archbishop of Cologne's] Diocese, that certain Heretics are apprehended by those who are most notorious for their errors in these days. These are those who are most commonly called Cathari; a race most pernicious to the Catholic faith, which, going about with great subtilty, they destroy like moths. They are furnished with words of Holy Scripture which seem in a certain way to countenance their sect, and by means of these they know how to defend their own errors, and abuse the Catholic faith. Of the right sense however which is contained in the words, and which is not to be come at without great discretion, they are extremely ignorant. I have therefore thought it worth while to describe their errors, and to set down the authorities of Scripture by which they defend themselves, and to shew their real meaning; and, at the same time, to state those parts of our faith which they oppose, and by the help of God to shew by what authorities of Scripture, and by what arguments, they may be defended, in order that those who read these things, and take pains to remember them, may be somewhat better prepared to dispute with these persons; if, as frequently happens, they shall be detected among the people. For they are very talkative, and are always prepared with what they have to say against us, and it is no small disgrace to us who are learned, that we should be mute and have nothing to say in reply to them. When I was a Canon in the church of Bonn, I and my like-minded friend Bertolphus frequently disputed with such persons, and I paid great attention to their errors and defences. Many things also concerning them became known by means of those who had left their sect, and had been delivered out of the snares of the devil. I have, therefore, by the exhortation of my Abbot, the Lord Hildelinus, put together in this book the more fully both their opinions, and what may be opposed to them; and I have sent it to your Highness (vestræ celsitudini) for old friendship's sake; so that if it should happen that such persons are examined before you, your prudence may be assisted by these discourses in stopping the mouths of those who speak wickedly, and in confirming the unstable minds of persons easily seduced; who, being deceived by their artful discourses, believe that they walk according to truth. I ask therefore that if you approve of this work, and foresee that it will be useful in any way to the Christian religion, you will cause it to be made public that it may be a stumbling block to that most wicked generation for all time to come . . . .

The Virgin Church hath received one pearl of great price as her dowry from Jesus Christ her spouse, namely, the Catholic faith; and this, alas! has in these days many enemies, who attempt its destruction. I believe that those perils of the last times have begun to come upon us, concerning which our Saviour prophesied in the Gospel; when, speaking to his disciples of the signs which should precede the day of judgment he said, according to St. Matthew, among other things, "Then if any one shall say, 'lo here is Christ' or 'lo there' believe it not, for there shall arise false Christs, and false prophets, and shall perform great signs, and wonders, so that if it were possible even the Elect shall be deceived; behold! I have foretold you; if therefore they shall say to you, 'Behold! he is here in the desert;' go not forth; 'Behold he is in the secret chambers,' believe it not." And, indeed, if hitherto any one hath come who was so insane as to call himself Christ, we have not heard of it; but concerning false prophets, who say that Christ is in the secret chambers, we now see much. For, behold, many persons affecting concealment, seduced and seducers, who for a long time have been hidden, and have secretly corrupted the Christian faith in many persons of foolish simplicity, are so multiplied in all lands, that the church of God suffers great danger from the most wicked poison which they pour forth against her on every side. For their discourse eats as doth a canker, and flies far and wide, like an infectious leprosy, contaminating the precious members of Christ. These are called with us in Germany *Cathari*, in Flanders *Piphles*, in France *Texerant*, because they are weavers. As our Lord predicted concerning them, they say that Christ is in the secret chambers; because they say that the true faith of Christ, and true worship of Christ, exist no where except in their conventicles, which they hold in cellars, in workshops, and such like under-ground places. They say that they lead the life of the Apostles, but they are contrary to the holy faith, and sound doctrine, which has been delivered to us by the holy Apostles, and by the Lord the Saviour himself. For they are the persons of whom St. Paul thus speaks, in his Epistle to Timothy, "Now the Spirit speaketh expressly, that in the latter times some shall depart from the faith, giving heed to seducing spirits, and doctrines of devils, speaking lies in hypocrisy, having their conscience seared with a hot iron, forbidding to marry, and commanding to abstain from meats, which God hath created to be received with thanksgiving." And truly these are they to whom this discourse belongs, since they reprobate and condemn marriage, so that they assign to those who remain until death in a state of marriage, nothing less than eternal damnation. Some of them, indeed, say that they approve of the marriage of those who are both virgins; but they say that even these cannot be saved unless they are separated before death, and by this also they forbid such marriage. They who have become *perfect* members of the sect avoid all flesh; not abstaining from the same reason as monks, and other persons living a religious life do, but they say that the eating of flesh is to be avoided on account of the means by which it is produced, and on account of which they consider it unclean; and this is the reason which they publicly give: but in secret they say what is worse—namely, that all flesh is made by the devil, and therefore they never taste it even in the greatest extremities. Concerning baptism they speak variously. They say that baptism profits nothing to children who are baptized, for they cannot seek baptism by themselves, because they can make no profession of faith. There is also another thing which they say more generally, but more privately—namely, that no water baptism is profitable to salvation; for which reason they re-baptize those who enter their sect, in a certain secret manner of their own; which baptism they say is done in the Holy Ghost and fire.

Concerning the souls of the dead they hold, that at the time of their death they pass either to everlasting blessedness, or to eternal damnation, for they do not receive what the universal Church believes—namely, that there are certain purgatorial punishments, in which the souls of some of the elect are for a time tried for their sins, from which they are not fully purified in this life by due satisfaction. On this account therefore they think it vain, and superfluous, to pray for the dead, to give alms, to say masses—and they ridicule the tolling of bells which we make, which is nevertheless done by our Church from pious motives, namely that the living may be admonished to pray for the dead, and be led to consider their own mortality.

They altogether despise, and consider as of no value, the masses which are celebrated in the Churches; for if it happens that they go with the rest of their neighbours to hear masses, or even to receive the eucharist, they do this in mere dissimulation lest their infidelity should be discovered. For they say that the order of the Priesthood is altogether lost in the Church of Rome, and in all the Churches of the Catholic faith, and the true Priests are not to be found except in their Sect. They believe that the body and blood of Christ can be by no means made by our consecration, or received by us in our communion; but they say that they alone make the body of Christ at their tables; but in those words there is this deceit—for they do not mean that true body of Christ which we believe to have been born of the Virgin, and to have suffered on the cross, but they call their own flesh the body of the Lord; and forasmuch as they nourish their bodies by the food on their tables, they say that they make the body of the Lord.

Nor will I pass over what I heard from a certain faithful man, who, having discovered their infidelity, and some secret wickednesses, left their Society; for he affirmed that they so erred respecting the Lord the Saviour as to say, that he was not truly born of the Virgin, nor had true human flesh, but only an appearance of flesh, and that he did not rise from the dead, but only pretended his death and resurrection. On which account, if they are among Christians who are celebrating Easter, they either conform in a negligent manner, or they seek occasions of being absent from their own home, lest they should be compelled to keep the feast with their neighbours. Instead of this however they celebrate another festival, in which their Heresiarch Manichæus was slain, whose heresy without doubt they follow, which St. Augustine, writing against the Manichæans says was called Bema. My informant, however, says that among those with whom he was connected, it was called *Malilosa*, and was celebrated in the Autumn.

Beside these things, we have discovered a new, and hitherto unheard of, madness of their's, which some of them when they were examined by the Clergy in the City of Cologne (where by the people full of fervent zeal they were burned) openly confessed—for they said that human souls were no other than those apostate spirits who in the beginning of the world were cast out of the Kingdom of Heaven, and that they might obtain salvation in human bodies, by means of good works; but this only among those who belonged to their Sect.

Such things as these they have for a long while privately whispered, going about everywhere to the houses of such persons as were liable to be seduced; and we have heard that these most wicked whisperers do in these times lead captive many unhappy souls in their bonds. They compass, if I may so speak, sea and land that they may make one Catharus, and asperse every other mode of religion by impious detraction, and affirm that no one can be saved unless he joins their sect. It is therefore necessary that all who have zeal for God and their senses exercised in the holy scriptures should watch with all diligence in order to take these most wicked little foxes which destroy the vineyard. Their errors indeed are so many that no one can number them; but I have distinguished and set in order those which appeared to me the most dangerous, because I intend by God's help to write against them in particular. . . .

[The following illustrates the Catharist rite of the *consolmentum*:]

I am not ignorant however that you hold as great a heresy concerning the baptism of Adults, as that which has now been discussed concerning infant-baptism; for you say, that a man is indeed to be baptized when he comes to years of discretion, not however in water, but in fire; and that the baptism of water is of no use to any body. You defend this error by the words which John spoke with reference to the Lord the Saviour; "He shall baptize you in the Holy Ghost and fire." Hence it is that those whom you receive into your Catharist Society (as I have heard from one who had been initiated into your mysteries) you re-baptize in the following manner—assembling yourselves in some obscure chamber, your first care is, lest there should be any window, or door, through which those who are without might see or hear what is going on within. Since it is written he that doeth evil hateth the light, lamps are placed in great numbers in all the walls. The company stand arranged in a circle, with great reverence, for they are engaged in a holy service, though certainly one more pleasing to the devil than to God. The unhappy person who is to be baptized; or Catharized, is placed in the middle, and the Archicatharus stands by him, holding in his hand a book appointed for this purpose. Placing it upon his head, he utters benedictions (which might more properly be called maledictions) while the rest of the company pray; and they make a child of hell, and not of the kingdom of God, and thus this baptism is performed. It is said moreover to be made in fire, on account of the fire of the lights which burn all around. . . .

[Here Eckbert describes the heretics' belief that Christ's physical body was only an illusion:]

It seems to me that I have been building a house without a foundation; for those who know you well say, that you deny the humanity of the Saviour. If it be so I have lost my time in disputing with you about the body and blood of the Lord. I can however believe, that the disciples of an insane teacher, may be themselves insane; for Manes, the leader of your error, taught that our Saviour so far appeared in human nature that he seemed to be, but was not truly, a man; and that he was not truly born of the Virgin, and did not truly suffer, or die, or rise from the dead," &c.

12   *Christine Thouzellier*
Catharisme et Valdéisme en Languedoc

*Catharism spread even more rapidly in southern Europe than in the north.
The following is taken from Christine Thouzellier,* Catharisme et Valdéisme en
Languedoc. *This is the conclusion of her book.*

At the end of the twelfth and the beginning of the thirteenth century
Catharism and Valdesianism developed in the south of France, around
Narbonne, in Catalonia, along the Rhône, along the Atlantic coast,
and in Périgord.

The soil was well prepared. The general opinion of the Church,
including popes, councils, theologians, chroniclers, and historians,
confirmed the reproaches of the heretics against the corruption of the
Church. The deterioration of Christian morality and the indifference
of a clergy often more eager to pursue luxury than humility facilitated
the expansion of the Reformist movements. The Reformist spirit of
independence and religious revival also drew strength from the rise
of the towns, which were attempting to obtain independence, and
from the need of the townspeople to escape from arbitrary domination at a time when economic development was leading them to claim
a certain autonomy.

To these spiritual and material causes was added a deep desire on
the part of individuals to understand the laws governing their fate.
Unsatisfied by the explanations offered them by an unconvincing
orthodoxy, the minds of men were open to the blandishments of a
view of the world that, however strange, seemed able to solve their
problems: the powerful view suggested by a new evangelical spirit.

Catharism and Valdesianism thus appeared in Languedoc with
diametrically opposed doctrines but with a view of the Church that,
although it sprang from totally different sources, was similar; contempt for the Church, for its ministers, and for its sacraments. Their
ethical teaching was more divergent: Catharism taught the denial of
life, while Valdesianism urged men to follow the spiritually creative

SOURCE. Christine Thouzellier, *Catharisme et Valdéisme en Languedoc* (Paris: Presses
Universitaires, 1966), pp. 425–427. Translated for this volume by Jeffrey B. Russell.
Reprinted by permission of the author.

teaching of the Gospels. Yet both these separate currents of thought attracted the faithful who felt disappointed in Roman Catholicism. Disturbed and at a loss to explain the human drama in which they were caught, they looked for a theology and a doctrine that seemed comprehensible, that promised them eternal security and that pointed out to them a way of obtaining salvation in this world.

Every group in society was touched by these heresies: the clergy and the laity, the nobles and the gentry, the merchants and the artisans, the townsfolk and the farmers, men and women.

The Catharists, adherents of a doctrine they considered certain, formed a church with its own hierarchy: believers grouped around bishops and *perfecti*. This Catharist Church formed an autonomous and formidable opposition to the Church of Rome and to Catholicism in general.

Less organized in Languedoc than the Catharists, the Valdesians, who were authentic Christians rather than dualists, were defenders of the Gospel. They rapidly attracted many adherents from among those who, though adhering to orthodoxy, were motivated by a spirit of independence. Because the Valdesians of Provence and Lombardy were in such close contact with other heretics, they ended by adopting some of the Catharist ideas at the expense of the pristine rectitude of their founder.

Swiftly the Catholic theologians sounded the alarm, seeking to demonstrate the basic irrationality of the two systems of heresy. The earlier Valdesians who still thought of themselves as orthodox entered the fray on the side of orthodoxy, combating the extreme dualists by their preaching and their writing. The close relations between the Catharists of Languedoc and those of Lombardy promoted the spread of heresy, strengthened its effect, and spread throughout the West oriental myths derived from the Greek, Bulgarian, and Balkan background of the Catharists. The Catharism of Languedoc derived from ancient Manicheism and Paulicianism with a touch of Bogomilism.

The spiritual forces which were sent to combat heresy in southern France were insufficient to the task. Debates, preaching, and good example eventually yielded to a papal policy (directed at Italy as well as at France) designed to deter heresy by legal proceedings against the liberty and the property of individuals. Indifferent to the threats of the popes, the heretics continued to engage in intensive propaganda to the point of forcing Innocent III to adopt drastic measures. To Innocent III the use of the temporal sword against the heretics

appeared to be inevitable. Although it was originally a plan to eradicate heresy in Lombardy, the crusade actually began in the area around
Narbonne. A motley army of crusaders, attracted as much by the
ambition of obtaining property as by the desire to win indulgences
(which were more quickly obtained by going to Languedoc than in the
long voyage to the Holy Land), poured into the County of Toulouse.
The army of Count Raymond of Toulouse gradually collapsed before
the attack of the Capetian king of France, Louis VII, but the Catharists
and the Valdesians remained active, and, supported by the population, hid in the forests, took refuge in the hills, or fled to peaks along
the frontier.

Thus, in spite of the crusade, the spirit of dissent was not extin-
guished. The Gospel spirit of Durand de Osca and the apostolic
vigor of Saint Dominic rallied the faint of heart and provoked a free
discussion that brought forth light. Debates did not cease, and one
of the more active debaters, Durand de Osca of Aragon, a converted
Valdesian, became their most important champion. His institute at
Elna assembled a collection of books, including relevant Biblical texts
and anti-Catharist documents. Adding to what he already had in the
material provided in the *Catharist Treaty* of his opponents, he published
his refutation of Catharism under the title of *The Book Against The
Manichaeans.*

In spite of the publication of this book, and in spite of the effort of
preachers and controversialists, it was the sword that was finally used
to vanquish the stubborn resistance of minds devoted to religious
liberty. The Treaty of Paris, formalizing the effects of the Albigensian
crusade, annexed Languedoc to the French crown. The establishment
of the Inquisition ended by forcing the stubborn into silence, and
repressing with physical force a movement properly in the realm of the
mind and of the spirit.

13   *Antoine Dondaine*
              La Hiérarchie cathare en Italie

*This document is entitled "De heresi catharorum in Lombardia," edited by Dondaine
in his article, "La hiérarchie cathare en Italie," Archivum Fratrum Praedicatorum.*

SOURCE. Father Antoine Dondare, O.P., ed., "De heresi catharorum in Lombardia,"
in Dondaine, "La hiérarchie cathare en italie," in *Archivum Fratrum Praedicatorum*, xix
(1949), pp. 280–312. Translated for this volume by Jeffrey B. Russell.

At the time when the heresy of the Catharists in Lombardy was beginning to spread for the first time, they had a bishop by the name of Mark . . . whose episcopal orders derived from Bulgaria. A certain priest, Nicheta, came from Constantinople into Lombardy and began to question Mark's orders. Therefore Bishop Mark with his followers, dubious of their own position, left the Bulgarian order and received from Nicheta the order of Drugonthia.[1] [There now follows a discussion of a schism within the Catharist Church in Lombardy between factions each claiming that it represented the legitimate Catharist hierarchy.]

The beliefs of one of the groups of Catharists, those who follow the order of Drugonthia[2] now follows: They believe and preach that there are two Gods or Lords without beginning and without end, one of them good and the other deeply evil; and they say that each God created angels, the good God the good angels and the bad God the bad angels, and that the good God is omnipotent in heaven, while the evil God has lordship over all of this world. And they say that Lucifer is the Son of the God of darkness, as it says in the Gospel of Saint John: "You are from your father the Devil. . . . " And they say that this Lucifer rose from his kingdom and ascended into Heaven. . . . And there he transformed himself into an angel of light. The other angels, admiring his beauty, interceded for him before the Lord, and he was taken up into heaven where he was made the overseer of the angels. . . . With this authority he seduced the other angels into evil. And then they say that there was a great battle in heaven, and that "that ancient serpent was cast down from heaven" with the angels that he had led astray. . . . And they say that the life of human bodies partly derives from the evil spirits that the Devil has created and partly from the spirits that have fallen from heaven. The souls of the fallen do penance in the body. If they cannot obtain salvation in one body, their soul enters into another body and does penance there. And when their penance has finally been done, their bodies and spirits go to heaven and remain there.

The teachings of the other group of Catharists[3] are as follows. They say that Lucifer and his companions sinned in heaven, but they are unsure what was the origin of this sin. Some of them say—this is difficult to understand—that it was the fault of a certain evil spirit

[1]A composite spelling referring to the churches of Dragovitsa and Tragurium.—Ed.
[2]The absolute dualists.—Ed.
[3]The "mitigated dualists."—Ed.

having four faces, one of a man, one of a bird, one of a fish, and one of an animal. This evil spirit had no beginning and dwelt in the primeval chaos, having no power of creating. And they say that Lucifer (who had been good until then) descended from heaven and, seeing the face of this evil spirit, admired it. After having conversed with this evil spirit and having been influenced by him, Lucifer was led astray. He returned to heaven where he led others astray, and finally he and his followers were cast out of heaven. They did not, however, lose their natural powers as angels. And these heretics say that Lucifer and the other evil spirit wanted to create a material universe but were unable to do so. But they won over to their side one of the angels who was a chief assistant of God, and with the help of this good angel and the permission of God, they created the material universe. The heretics say that this Lucifer is the God who is said in the Book of Genesis to have created heaven and earth and to have done these things in six days. And they say that this Lucifer made Adam out of mud and in the form of Adam choked the good angel to death. . . . And he made Eve and caused Adam to sin through her. And they say that what was meant by the eating of the forbidden fruit was fornication.

The common opinion of all the Catharists is that all the things that are spoken of in the Book of Genesis about the flood, about the sparing of Noah, about God's covenant with Abraham, and about the destruction of Sodom and Gomorrah—all these things were deeds done by the Devil, who is called "God" in the Old Testament. And this God led the people out of Egypt and gave them the Law in the desert and led them into the Promised Land and sent them prophets— all for the purpose of being worshipped as God, causing the Jewish people at the instigation of the prophets to offer him blood sacrifice. And if the Jewish prophets at any time predicted anything about the Christ who was to come, it was not through their free will but rather through the action of the Holy Spirit. And they claim that Almighty God did all these deeds not through himself but through the Devil acting for him as his minister. Thus they claim that whatever the Devil did was done with the authority and the strength and the power that God delegated to him and that he did all of these things with the permission of God. It was the Devil's plan in all this to rule the world, though the true God had of course another intention, that of achieving goodness and the salvation of souls through their penitence. . . .

They say that Christ did not really take on the flesh, that he did not eat or drink, nor was he crucified nor did he die, nor was he buried, and all things that he did according to human nature were not truly done but only in appearance. . . .

They say that John the Baptist was sent by the Devil and that baptism was established in order to hinder the teaching of Christ. . . . All of the Catharists condemn marriage and deny the Resurrection of the Body. They all say that baptism with water is of no use whatsoever to salvation. . . .

14   *Antoine Dondaine*
Un Traité néo-manichéen du XIIIe siècle

The following are selections from two of the few documents actually composed by the Catharists themselves, the Liber de Duobus Principibus *("Book of the Two Principles") and a Catharist* Rituale *or handbook of rituals. These were first fully edited by Father Antoine Dondaine, O.P., in* Un traité néo-manichéen du XIIIe siècle.

FROM THE SECTION OF THE "BOOK" ENTITLED
"THE INSTRUCTION OF THE SIMPLE"

On the Principle of Evil.   It is to be firmly believed by the wise that there is another principle of evil, powerful in iniquity, from whom Satan and all the other evil powers who oppose the true God derive their strength. . . . For otherwise the wise would have to believe that the true divine power is struggling and fighting with itself. . . .

On the alien God and the many gods.   If anyone should doubt what we have said, let him grasp the fact that there is another God and lord aside from the true God and lord. . . . There are many gods and lords and powers opposed to the true God and to his son Jesus Christ, as the Scriptures themselves testify. . . .

That the creator of the universe is not the true God but the other God.   It is perfectly clear from Scriptures that the God and Lord who is the creator of the world is different from him to whom the blessed commend their spirits. . . . Our opponents [i.e., the Catholics] say

SOURCE. *Liber de Duobus Principibus*, in Father Antoine Dondaine, O.P., ed., *Un traité néo-manichéen du XIIIe siècle* (Rome: Istituto storico dominicano, 1939), pp. 121–128. Translated for this volume by Jeffrey B. Russell.

that according to Genesis the lord is the creator of the visible things of this world: the heaven and the earth, the sea, men and beasts, birds and reptiles. . . . But I say that the creator of the visible things of this world is not the true God. And I prove this from the evil of his words and deeds, and the changeableness of his words and deeds as described in the old Testament. . . . [There follows a discussion of the morally questionable actions of God as described in the Old Testament. The Catharists, it will be observed, were offering one answer to the old problem of reconciling the existence of God with the existence of evil: evil was to be attributed to the evil God, not to the true God.] It is evident enough to the wise that the true God could not be this creator who mercilessly tempts men and women to destruction. . . .

A DESCRIPTION OF THE *CONSOLAMENTUM* IN THE "BOOK OF RITUAL"

Then the officiant shall take the book from the hands of the believer and say: "John (if that indeed is his name), do you wish to receive this holy baptism of Jesus Christ . . . and to keep it your whole life long in purity of heart and mind; and not to fall in any manner into sin?" And John shall reply: "Yes, I do. Call upon the good God for me that he may give me his grace." And the officiant shall say: "May the true lord God grant you the grace to receive this gift to his honor and to your own welfare." Then the believer shall stand reverently before the officiant and say, along with the acolyte: "I have come before you and before God and before the Church and before your holy order for the purpose of receiving pardon and forgiveness for all my sins from the beginning until now. Pray that God may grant me this. Bless us; have mercy on us." Then shall the officiant reply: "May you receive pardon and mercy for all your sins from God, from the Church, from God's sacred order, from his precepts and his disciples, and may the lord God of mercy forgive you and receive you into life everlasting." And the believer shall say: "Amen, may it be done unto us, o Lord, according to your will." Then shall the believer rise and in front of the officiant place his hands upon the Gospels. And the

SOURCE. *Rituale*, in Father Antoine Dondaine, O.P., ed., *Un traité néo-marichéen du XIIIe siècle* (Rome: Istituto storico dominicano, 1939). pp. 164–165. Translated for this volume by Jeffrey B. Russell.

officiant shall then place the book upon the believer's head, and all the other elect and other Christians who shall be there shall place their right hands upon his head. And the officiant shall say: "In the name of the Father and the Son and the Holy Spirit." And he who is receiving the *consolamentum* shall say: "Amen." And all the others shall say clearly: "Amen." Then shall the officiant say: "Bless you and keep you. Amen. Let it be done unto us, Lord, according to your will. May the Father and the Son and the Holy Spirit send you away in peace, having forgiven you your sins. Let us worship the Father and the Son and the Holy Spirit [three times]: Holy Father, the true, the just, and the merciful, now send away your servant in peace and receive him into your justice. Our Father [the Lord's prayer follows]".
. . . And he shall say aloud five prayers and then the "Let us worship" three times. And then he shall say one prayer and then again the "Let us worship" three times. Then he shall read the beginning of the Gospel According to John: "In the beginning was the Word," and so on. When the Gospel has been read, he shall again say three times the "Let us worship," and then another prayer. And then again three times the "Let us worship," and he shall offer a benediction. And the Christian [i.e., he who is receiving the *consolamentum*] shall kiss the book and then bow three times, saying: "Bless, bless, bless, spare us; may God grant you a good reward for the good that you have done me for the love of God." Then shall the elect, the Christian men, and the Christian women receive the *servicium* [the general Catharist service of confession and absolution] according to the custom of the Church.

May all good Christians pray to God for him who has written these rules. Amen. Thanks be to God.

PART IV

Heresy and Intellectual Movements

Although the most important doctrinal disputes had been settled before the Middle Ages, changes in the intellectual climate provoked new questions or new approaches to old ones. When this occurred, theological controversy arose, and often those who were defeated in these controversies were accused of heresy. Periods of rapid intellectual change were therefore more likely to produce intellectual heresy than others. Thus during the so-called "Carolingian Renaissance" controversies over the eucharist and predestination arose. In the eleventh and twelfth centuries the new methods of scholasticism and the Greek and Arab ideas introduced through translations produced a revolution in theology, a revolution some of whose leading exponents, like Abelard and Gilbert de la Porrée, were condemned by conservatives as heretics. Again, during the break-up of scholasticism at the end of the thirteenth and at the beginning of the fourteenth century, theological unrest produces accusations of heresy against Siger, Ockham, and others.

15   *Abelard*

Abelard (d. 1142) was one of the originators of the scholastic method. He offended many people in positions of power, notably St. Bernard, by his personal arrogance and by his insistence that reason was superior to tradition in the resolution of theological questions. One of his most controversial works was Sic et Non—"Yes and No"—*in which he listed a number of theological questions and cited Church Fathers on both sides, leaving it to the reader to draw the conclusion that an appeal to tradition alone did not suffice to solve the problems. Abelard's confidence in his own brilliant use of reason to explore theological problems not only antagonized ecclesiastical leaders but led him to formulate a number of propositions that were condemned as heretical at the Council of Sens in 1140.*

The opposition of William of Saint-Thierry, St. Bernard, and others to Abelard's ideas led to the condemnation of nineteen propositions ascribed to Abelard at the council of Sens. Some of these propositions are actually not found in Abelard's own works at all. Most of them are but were taken out of context. It is not clear precisely what the council really considered heretical about these propositions, or whether they were seized upon as a convenient weapon to use against a man who had offended many of the leading theologians of his day.

---

a. The Nineteen Capitula

1. Quod Pater sit plena potentia, Filius quaedam potentia, Spiritus Sanctus nulla potentia.

That the Father is full power; the Son partial (literally, a certain) power; the Holy Spirit, no power.

2. Quod Spiritus Sanctus non sit de substantia Patris aut Filii.

That the Holy Spirit is not of the substance of the Father or the Son.

3. Quod Spiritus Sanctus sit anima mundi.

That the Holy Spirit is the world-soul.

4. Quod Christus non assumpsit carnem, ut nos a jugo dyaboli liberaret.

That Christ did not assume the flesh in order to liberate us from the yoke of the devil.

SOURCE. J. G. Sikes, *Peter Abailard*, New York: Russell & Russell, 1965.

5. Quod neque Deus et homo, neque haec persona quae Christus est, sit tertia persona in Trinitate.

That neither the man-God, nor that person who is Christ, is the third person in the Trinity.

6. Quod liberum arbitrium per se sufficiat ad aliquid bonum.

That free will in and of itself suffices for some good.

7. Quod ea solummodo Deus possit facere vel dimittere, vel eo modo tantum, vel eo tempore quo facit, non alio.

That God can only do or forego doing things, in the manner or at the time that he does, and not otherwise.

8. Quod Deus nec debeat nec possit mala impedire.

That God ought not and cannot prevent evil.

9. Quod non traximus culpam ex Adam, sed poenam tantum.

That we do not get guilt from Adam, but only punishment.

10. Quod non peccaverunt, qui Christum ignorantes crucifixerunt, et quod non sit culpae ascribendum quidquid fit per ignor-
antiam.

That they who crucified Christ, in ignorance, did not sin and whatever is done in ignorance is not to be ascribed to guilt.

11. Quod in Christo non fuerit spiritus timoris Domini.

That in Christ there was no spirit of fear of the Lord.

12. Quod potestas ligandi atque solvendi apostolis tantum data sit, non et successoribus eorum.

That the power of binding and loosing was given only to the apostles, and not to their successors.

13. Quod propter opera nec peior nec melior efficiatur.

That works do not make a man better or worse.

14. Quod ad Patrem, qui ab alio non est, proprie vel specialiter attineat omnipotentia, non etiam et sapientia et benignitas.

That omnipotence, but not wisdom and goodness, properly and specially pertains to the Father, who does not derive his being from another.

15. Quod etiam castus timor excludatur a futura vita.

That even holy fear is excluded from the future life.

16. Quod dyabolus immittat suggestiones per appositionem lapidum vel herbarum.

That the devil makes suggestions through the application of precious stones or herbs. [Abelard subscribed to an old and common belief that diabolical power could be brought to bear through the swallowing of certain herbs or the use of certain stones as pendants.]

17. Quod adventus in fine saeculi possit attribui Patri.

That the second coming at the end of the world can be attributed to the Father.

18. Quod anima Christi per se non descendit ad inferos, sed per
potentiam tantum.

That the soul of Christ did not itself descend into hell, but only
its power.

19. Quod neque opus neque voluntas neque concupiscentia, neque
delectatio quae movet eam, peccatum sit, nec debemus eam velle
extingui.

Not act or will, nor desire or the pleasure that arouses it, is a sin,
and we should not wish it to be suppressed.

*b. This letter of Saint Bernard to Rome indicates the degree to which Abelard
had aroused opposition.*

LETTER 238
TO THE BISHOPS AND CARDINALS IN CURIA

To the lords and reverend fathers, the Bishops and Cardinals in
Curia, from the child of their holiness.

No one has any doubt that it belongs especially to you to remove
scandals from the Kingdom of God, to cut back the growing thorns,
to calm quarrels. For this is what Moses commanded when he went
up the mountain, saying: "Wait here till we come back to you. You
have Aaron and Hur with you; to them refer all matters of dispute."
I speak of that Moses who came through water, and "not by water only,
but by water and blood".[1] And therefore he is greater than Moses
because he came through blood. And because by Aaron and Hur the
zeal and authority of the Roman Church are signified, I do well to
refer to her, not questions about the faith, but wounds to the faith,
injuries to Christ, insults and dishonours to the Fathers, the scandals
of the present generation and the dangers of those to come. The
faith of the simple is being held up to scorn, the secrets of God
are being reft open, the most sacred matters are being recklessly
discussed, and the Fathers are being derided because they held that

SOURCE. Bruno Scott James, *The Letters of Saint Bernard of Clairvaux* (Chicago: Henry
Regnery Company, 1953), pp. 315–317. Reprinted by permission of the publisher.

[1] "This is he that came by water and blood, Jesus Christ; not by water only but by
water and blood." (1 *John* 5.6).

such matters are better allowed to rest[2] than solved. Hence it comes about that, contrary to the law of God, the Paschal Lamb is either boiled or eaten raw, with bestial mouth and manners.[3] And what is left over is not burned with fire, but trodden under foot.[4] So mere human ingenuity is taking on itself to solve everything, and leave nothing to faith. It is trying for things above itself, prying into things too strong for it, rushing into divine things, and profaning rather than revealing what is holy. Things closed and sealed, it is not opening but tearing asunder, and what it is not able to force open, that it considers to be of no account and not worthy of belief.

2. Read, if you please, that book of Peter Abelard which he calls a book of Theology. You have it to hand since, as he boasts, it is read eagerly by many in the Curia. See what sort of things he says there about the Holy Trinity, about the generation of the Son, about the procession of the Holy Spirit, and much else that is very strange indeed to Catholic ears and minds. Read that other book which they call the *Book of Sentences*,[5] and also the one entitled *Know Thyself*, and see how they too run riot with a whole crop of sacrileges and errors. See what he thinks about the soul of Christ, about the person of Christ, about his descent into hell, about the Sacrament of the Altar, about the power of binding and loosing, about original sin, about the sins of human weakness, about the sins of ignorance, about sinful action, and about sinful intention. And if you then consider that I am rightly disturbed, do you also bestir yourselves and, so as not to bestir yourselves in vain, act according to the position you hold, according to the dignity in which you are supreme, according to the power you have received, and let him who has scanned the heavens go down even into hell, and let the works of darkness that have braved the light be shown up by the light, so that while he who sins in public is publicly rebuked, others, who speak evil in their hearts and write it in their

[2] . . . *quod eas magis sopiendas, quam solvendas censuerint*. Eales, apparently understanding *sopiendas* as *sapiendas* translates: '. . . because they held that such things are rather to be tasted than solved'.

[3] . . . *more et ore bestiali*.

[4] "No part must be eaten raw, or boiled, it must be roasted over the fire . . . whatever is left over, you must put in the fire and burn it" (*Exodus* 12.9).

[5] Abelard denied that he had ever written a book with this name and implied that St. Bernard could not distinguish between Peter Lombard and himself. But Bernard was familiar with the works of Peter Lombard, and also his *Book of Sentences* was not published when this letter was written. Undoubtedly he is referring here to Abelard's book *Sic et Non* which starts: "Here begin sentences taken from the Holy Scriptures which seem opposed to each other . . .'

books, may restrain themselves from putting darkness for light, and disputing on divine matters at the crossroads. Thus shall the mouth that mutters wickedness be closed.

16   *Amalric of Bena*
                              Contra Amaurianos

Amalric was a professor at the University of Paris whose beliefs were posthumously condemned at Paris in 1210 as heretical. He had followers, called Amalricians, who mingled with Amalric's intellectual pantheism the more popular belief that men are justified by the Spirit within. Pantheism and Reformism thus reinforced one another. The following Amalrician ideas are taken from the treatise Contra Amaurianos *(Against the Amalricians).*

God is everywhere.
God is in other places besides being in himself.
God is in time.
All things are in the essence of God.
One who knows that God is working within him is incapable of sinning.
Hell is nothing other than being ignorant.
Heaven is understanding the truth.

If a Jew should understand the truth as we understand it, it would not be necessary (to his salvation) to baptize him.

If a person understands the truth, he need not perform a long penance assigned him by a priest.

To understand the truth is the only kind of resurrection there will be.

No one can be saved unless he believe himself a member of Christ.

God is all things in all things (*Deus est omnia in omnibus*). The Father was incarnate in Abraham and in the other patriarchs; the Son was incarnate in Christ and in other Christians; and the Holy Spirit in the "spirituals" [i.e., those who understand the truth].

The Body of the Lord is everywhere.

SOURCE. *Contra Amaurianos*, in G. C. Capelle, *Autour du décret de 1212* (Paris: Vrin, 1932), pp. 90–91. Translated for this volume by Jeffrey B. Russell.

Just as the Body of the Lord is adored in the consecrated bread on the altar, so it should be adored in the everyday bread that is eaten. In five years all men will be "spirituals."

17   *Joachim of Flora*

Joachim was a mystical, millennarian teacher of the late-twelfth century. He believed that there were three ages of the world, that of the Father (before Christ), that of the Son (since the Incarnation), and that of the Holy Spirit, which would soon begin. The idea that men would soon be purified by the Spirit within influenced the Amalricians, and Joachism, like the Amalrician doctrines, aided the growth of beliefs of interior illumination and their influence on Reformism.

The following is taken from Gordon Leff, Heresy in the Later Middle Ages.

For Joachim the years from 1200 to 1260 were to be the culmination of the change from the second to the third age. On the one hand they would be ones of "great tribulation," reaching a final crescendo with the advent of the first Antichrist to mark the end of the second era. While in a general sense, of course, the seventh age would inaugurate a new era of peace, the tribulations leading up to its consummation would become progressively more intense. In Joachim's words: "One thing we can say with certainty: the sixth age will be worse than the previous five ages, and the seventh age will be worse than the sixth, and both will be filled with the evil doings of the dragon of the Apocalypse." The sixth age, especially, would witness great persecutions culminating, in the seventh, with the appearance of the first Antichrist. On the other hand, the sixth age would also bring the first heralding of the spiritual understanding of the old and New Testaments which Gerard of Borgo San Donnino took for the everlasting gospel. This would come with the opening of the sixth of the seven seals of the holy book foretold by St. John of the Apocalypse. Joachim usually placed its occurrence during the fortieth generation of the second era, i.e. after 1200; but as the Anagni commission, which examined his works, justly complained, his words also implied the end of the forty-

SOURCE. Gordon Leff, *Heresy in the Later Middle Ages* (Manchester: Manchester University Press, 1967), pp. 72–74. Reprinted by permission of the publisher and the author.

second generation. In the beginning of the forty-second generation the Jews would be converted and the schism between the Greek and Latin churches healed. Joachim also envisaged their union under a final great Roman pontiff, the leader of the New Jerusalem in its struggle with Babylon. But he never developed the notion, as the later Joachists would, of an angelic pope. With the opening of the seventh seal God's mystery would be finished. Henceforth, after the vanquishing of Antichrist by the rider on the white horse, who Joachim surmised would be the reincarnated Christ, the rest of time would belong to the third age. A period of sabbatical peace would then reign, the era of those who would love God in "joy and solemnity." The peace of the seventh age would be finally broken by the coming of the second Antichrist—Gog—followed by Christ's second advent, the ending of the world, and the Last Judgement.

In the third place, however, the highly schematic nature of Joachim's thinking, far from engendering a world of abstractions, was fertile in allusions to the contemporary one. Here we must distinguish between their significance for Joachim and for the Joachists of subsequent generations. There can be no doubt that the focus of Joachim's attention was upon the transition from the second to the third state, namely the sixth and seventh epochs of the second state. Their symbolization in the sixth and seventh seals of the book of the Apocalypse formed the key to his outlook. It was only with their opening that the book could be read; and this could only be done by the lamb, i.e. through the coming of Christ. Once achieved, the barrier between true spiritual illumination and knowledge and the letter would be down; the third age would begin. Here Joachim effectively stopped. The third age was conceived less in itself than as the consummation of the second age; all the elements were already in existence: they merely had to reach full fructification. In this sense it can be truly said that Joachim conceived history "not in a single pattern of 'threes' but in two co-existing patterns, one of 'twos' and the other of 'threes'"; and more specifically as a series of parallels between the transitions from one status to the next.

It was in inspiring others to seek the vehicles for these changes that Joachim was to have such an impact; for this endowed his own predominantly symbolic—even poetic conception—of spiritual revelation with the seeds of an historicism. When these began to ripen in the later thriteenth century, Joachism germinated into perhaps the most challenging alternative to the existing dispensation which the later middle ages was to know.

The reasons are not far to seek. To begin with, there was the analogy between the ending of the first and second ages. Just as the first was transformed into the second by Christ, and personified in the order of clerics, so the second would culminate in the third with triumph of the new order of monks, who would personify it, over the forces of Antichrist. As Christ represented a qualitative change from his predecessors, so would the spiritual monks over theirs. This would consist above all in the supersession of action by contemplation, and would distinguish the seventh age of the second era from the sixth.

18   *Jeffrey B. Russell*
                    The Brethren of the Free Spirit

The Brothers and Sisters of the Free Spirit formed a loosely constructed group of sects during the thirteenth and fourteenth centuries, especially in the Rhineland and central Germany. The origins of their doctrines lie in part in Catharist dualism, in part in Reformism, and in part with the pantheism of Amalric of Bena, a professor at the University of Paris whose works were condemned as heretical in 1210. The first appearance of the Heresy of the Free Spirit may have been the sect of the Ortlibians. Ortlieb, a shadowy personality, is described by several documents of the thirteenth century as a bourgeois of Strasbourg with the office of *Schoeffe* or *scultetus*, that is to say a magistrate or at least a man of some public position. He was condemned as a heretic in 1216 by Pope Innocent III.

This is all that is known of Ortlieb, and there is little known of the sect of the Ortlibians, except that they are mentioned in a manuscript of Karlsruhe and appear as "Ortolini" in the condemnation of heretics issued by the emperor Frederick II in 1224. In spite of the sparseness of information, some historians have insisted on treating them as separate from the Brethren of the Free Spirit, even while they use as a source for the doctrines of Ortlieb the same source upon which they rely most heavily for the doctrines of the Free Spirit: the manuscript of the Passauer Anonymous. Rather, the Ortlibians should be considered an early appearance of the Brethren of the Free Spirit. There is no evidence for any organizational connection between the

SOURCE. Original article written for this volume.

Ortlibians and other Brethren, but this is not surprising, for the diversity of beliefs and actions among the Brethren indicates that they never were an organized or united sect.

The connection of the Brethren with the followers of Amalric of Bena, who were called Amalricians, can be established by two means: first by external evidence, establishing their geographical and temporal connection; and second by internal evidence, examining the affinity of their doctrines.

On the basis of external evidence alone, this connection cannot be definitely established. A similar social basis existed for the development of Amalric's ideas in France and Germany: both the Amalricians and the Brethren flourished in towns in which the bourgeois patricians had gained control and in which the artisans were in the process of asserting their rights against the patricians. It is not possible to generalize about the social class of the Brethren, however. Ortlieb was an established bourgeois; one chronicler says that the Brethren included monks, priests, and married people; another describes them as laborers, charcoal burners, blacksmiths, and swineherds; and yet another indicates that they were rough and illiterate men. It is most likely that the majority were of groups exercising little political or economic power: peasants, salaried laborers, poor artisans, and lower clergy. Marxist historians have somewhat exaggerated the elements of class warfare here, but the doctrines of the Brethren do clearly indicate that social protest was involved. For instance, they believed that a handmaiden or a servant could take and sell his master's goods without his permission. That tithes need not be paid to the Church is also a doctrine indicative of more than strictly theological discontent. The Brethren, like many Reformists of the thirteenth century, drew deeply from the new emphasis upon the holiness of poverty that had so strongly influenced both monastic and heretical movements (the Franciscans and Waldensians for example) since the later twelfth century.

The Reformist elements in the teaching of the Brethren are clear, but the connection with pantheism is also likely. The Amalricians were active in the area of Troyes and Langres in France, directly contiguous with the area in Germany where the Brethren of the Free Spirit were soon at work (Metz, Kolmar, Trier, Strasbourg) and where the valley of the Moselle provided easy access to the Rhineland from Champagne. Moreover, there were Brethren of the Free Spirit at Lyon (where the Waldensians were founded) in 1223: the sect was therefore operating at the termini of the trade route between the Saône-Rhone system and the middle Rhine at a time when the Amalricians were active along the same route, in Champagne.

In point of time, the Amalricians were condemned first in 1210 and again in 1215, and they were active at least as late as 1220, whereas Ortlieb was condemned in 1216; in 1215 some Brethren of the Free Spirit were among eighty burned at Strasbourg, and in 1216 again the Free Spirit was active in Alsace and Thurgau. At the same time the Waldensians and Catharists were active throughout western Europe and in far greater number than the Amalricians. The external evidence would indicate that the Brethren arose at a time and place—western Germany in the early thirteenth century—where a variety of heresies were active and where they had the opportunity of drawing their doctrines from a number of different sources.

An investigation of their doctrines, that is, the internal evidence, bears this out. The beliefs of the Brethren represent a blend of Reformist heresy with pantheism derived from the Amalricians, the most important common ingredient being the belief that the individual Christian is justified by the Holy Spirit dwelling within him and that it is from within, rather than from the institutional Church, that all grace proceeds.

Many of the teachings of the Brethren bear a very close resemblance to those of Amalric and his followers. God is formally all that is; every creature is God; the soul is of the substance of God. These were the cardinal tenets of Amalric and they became the basic principles of the Brethren of the Free Spirit. Since they are God, the Brethren maintained, like the Amalricians, they are in fact the Holy Spirit, and they ought to ignore all exterior pressures to follow the urgings of the Holy Spirit from within. Since the Brethren are the Holy Spirit, they cannot sin. A man can perform a sinful act without being in sin, and as long as he acts with the intention of following the will of the Spirit, his action is good.

These tenets, which the Amalricians had already held, were developed further by the Brethren of the Free Spirit. Since God is in all things, all bread is equally Christ and there is no need of consecration: the Brethren did no reverence to the Host. There is no hell or purgatory, and people can reach on earth a perfection as great as the blessed in heaven. In this they follow the Amalricians directly, and there is also a striking similarity to Amalrician teaching in their statement that Jews and pagans can be saved without baptism.

The final point in which there is complete correlation with the Amalricians is the belief in the three epochs taught by Joachim of

Flora. The millennarian teachings of the Italian abbot, which had proved for the Amalricians so congenial a supplement to the lofty pantheism of Amalric, proved a useful justification of their pneumatic doctrines for the Brethren. Joachim had predicted that the Third Age, the age of the Spirit, would soon arrive as a period of spiritual happiness on earth made possible by the indwelling of the Holy Spirit. For the Brethren, this age had come, and they were its heralds. These Joachist ideas did not have the prominence in the thought of the Brethren that one might have expected, however, possibly because their full development by Joachim was too complex and intellectual to be fully assimilated by their largely untutored minds.

Besides these points of belief in which there is complete correlation between the Amalricians and the Brethren of the Free Spirit, there are many other doctrines that are similar in both groups. The Brethren argued that since they were God, they had created everything and, united with God, ruled the universe. Sometimes the Brethren equated themselves with the Holy Spirit, and sometimes with Christ. A man who is united with God is to be revered as the very Body of Christ. There is no need of divine illumination to reach God. Some went beyond the limits of strict pantheism to argue that they were better than the saints, the Virgin, even than Christ, and that they were equal to God the Father. They despised churches and cemeteries, since God is in all places equally.

All things are God, so there is no evil, for "in every evil is the glory of God made manifest." They observed that men occasionally do sin and explained this phenomenon by concluding that when a man sinned the Holy Ghost left him, the Devil taking the place of the Paraclete in his soul. Had they carried their doctrines to their logical end, they might have observed that this was not a satisfactory solution, for in a pantheist universe the Devil must also be God. This refinement was not lost upon the Luciferans of the next century.

The ethical ideas that emerged from these doctrines involved those errors most likely to bring trouble to their proponents. They are God and therefore need obey no law, for St. Paul had written that "The law is not made for a righteous man" and that "If ye are led of the Spirit, ye are not under the law." The practice of virtue is not becoming to a man who is God since everything he does is good, and for the same reason penance and confession are not necessary, and the Ten Commandments and the precepts of the Church are not to be followed. Prayer is unnecessary, since man is God; fasting is likewise superfluous. Thieving is permissible, since if all things are God everything is held in common. Lying and perjury are not sinful. In their sexual mores the Brethren were no less unconventional. Fornication is no sin, nor, they added somewhat superfluously, is kissing. Oddly, they had their doubts about adultery, possibly because of experiences with irate husbands. Sex is bad if one does not feel impelled to the act by the urgings of the Spirit within, but if the urge is felt, then the act should be performed, no matter with whom.

Side by side with license are found doctrines of more strict or conventional morality. All did not fail to revere the Host, for example, but only some. Some did not go to confession at all; some went and simply said: "I have sinned." You may lie and commit perjury, but only if you are a "good man," said some; others strictly forbade all lying and oaths. Some Brethren argued that they were sinless; others admonished their brothers to avoid habitual sins.

This strange duality was not peculiar to the Brethren of the Free Spirit but has frequently been observed among the Catharists. Part of the explanation lies in the lack of organization and homogeneity among the Brethren: some groups and individuals were inclined one way, and some another. It is possible, however, that Catharist influence may among some groups have caused a division into something like the Catharist *credentes* and *perfecti*. This possibility is strengthened by the confession of one of the Brethren that he had practiced extreme asceticism, prayer, meditation, and almsgiving until he reached perfection. Then everything was permitted, and he committed hideous crimes of theft, murder, and perjury. The Amalricians, too, had maintained that, while in the future everyone would recognize that he was the Holy Spirit and be saved, presently not everyone was aware of his divine essence, and indeed salvation consisted in such a recognition and damnation in the failure to make such a recognition. It is therefore possible that the Brethren sometimes divided themselves into two groups, the novices practicing asceticism until a point, possibly not very far along, where they recognized the strivings of the Holy Spirit within them, and from that time forward they were free to do as they chose. If such a division ever occurred, it would be the opposite of the Catharist progression from laxness to asceticism.

The pantheist elements in the thought of the Brethren were clearly reinforced, if not by Catharist, certainly by Reformist, beliefs. That the Church is vanity and the clergy and pope useless, that no obedience is due to the Church of Rome, that the pope is the Whore of Babylon, were tenets held by the Waldensians, the Fraticelli, and other Reformists as well as by the Brethren. The Reformist influence seems particularly strong in such statements as the following: a priest is merely a preacher, twenty Pater Nosters are worth more than a Mass, prayers for the dead are useless, we are to use our own judgment in interpreting Scripture, and prayers in Latin are unintelligible to the people and therefore useless. The crucifix is an object, not of honor, but of detestation, an illumined layman is better than a bad priest, and everyone can consecrate the body and blood of Christ.

Occasionally a doctrine is mentioned that may betray Catharist influence: Christ suffered only for himself or did not suffer at all; unless a woman bewails the loss of her virginity in marriage she is damned (though St. Jerome himself might be responsible for that one); but the connections of Catharism with the Free Spirit are tenuous at best.

19　　　　*William Cornelius*

The following is an extract from the work (about 1252) of Thomas de Cantimpré, Bonum universale de apibus. *The translation is by Jeffrey B. Russell. Cantimpré's account of William Cornelius illustrates the persistence of the Reformist spirit in the thirteenth century.*

And in our time at Antwerp in Brabant one William Cornelius attempted to rend the seamless robe of Christ with an exceedingly irrational heresy. He resigned a prebendary benefice he had long occupied with the excuse that he wished henceforth to practice absolute poverty: but in point of fact he was wholly given over to lust. He said that just as fire consumes chaff, so poverty would consume every sin and annul guilt in the eyes of God. He argued that it was better to be a penurious whore than a perfectly chaste person living on a private income and that because of this all members of monastic orders are damned. His statement that lust is not a sin for poor people is an enormous blasphemy, for by so arguing he sets himself up as juster than the God of justice himself, who said, "You shall not favor

SOURCE. Thomas de Cantimpré, *Bonum universale de apibus* (about 1252), book 2, chapter 47. Translated for this volume by Jeffrey B. Russell.

the poor over others in your judgments." We have also learned by certain authority a curious story about this man. When he had died and been buried in the Church of the Blessed Virgin, a certain person, going into the church on the third day thereafter, saw with his own eyes a vision: the tomb of William Cornelius was open and empty. This was a manifestly significant presage of his future damnation, for, four years later, when the worthlessness and viciousness of his heresy was discovered, exposed, and proved, his body was exhumed by our venerable father Nicholas, bishop of Cambrai, and it was burned like a useless stalk, as Isaish said of Nebuchadnezzar.

William of Ockham

Ockham's skepticism as to the ability of human reason to arrive at absolute theological truth was a manifestation of the crisis in scholasticism at the end of the thirteenth century. The following is taken from Leff.

In intellectual matters there was a parallel development to that in spiritual life. From the last decade or so of the thirteenth century there was a movement away from the attempt to furnish a natural theology from the application of natural knowledge to the truths of revelation. It was given fullest expression by William of Ockham (d. 1349). He denied that knowledge drawn from natural experience could demonstrate or support the tenets of faith. He and his followers, like Robert Holcot (d. 1349), Thomas Buckingham (d. 1351), Adam of Woodham (d. 1357), John of Mirecourt, and Nicholas of Autrecourt as well as more orthodox contemporaries like Gregory of Rimini (d. 1358) refused to conceive Christian beliefs in created terms: or rather to try to adduce one from the other. Revealed truth was a matter of faith and was beyond the reach of natural understanding. Thus the existence of God, his nature, his actions, creation in time and *ex nihilo*, the requisites of salvation, were the province of faith and should remain such. Conversely, knowledge derived from this world should

SOURCE. Gordon Leff, *Heresy in the Later Middle Ages* (Manchester: Manchester University Press, 1967), pp. 294–297. Reprinted by permission of the publisher and the author.

be treated in natural and physical terms. The effect was to separate theology from the vast corpus of metaphysics and science which had come to the West via the Arabs. It was to abandon the task of assimilating them into a Christian framework, which had been perhaps the dominant theme of thirteenth-century thinking. Indeed, there was an almost obsessive awareness of the chasm between knowledge of God and knowledge of creation. Where God, as supreme being, was both necessary and free, creation was merely contingent, devoid of any inherent *raison d'être* beyond God's willing. On the one hand there was God, eternal and uncaused; on the other his creatures, who could as well have never been. This attitude helped to transform the intellectual attitude of the fourteenth century towards both God and creation.

So far as God was concerned the new element was the emphasis upon his freedom and his consequent unpredictability. It rested upon the time-honoured distinction between his two kinds of power: his absolute power (*potentia absoluta*) and his ordained power (*potentia ordinata*). By God's ordained power it was accepted that there was an inviolable order which he had decreed for this world and to which it was subject. It had been made known through God's word in the bible, the teaching of the *sancti* and the canons of the church. It was enshrined in the sacramental life of the church. By contrast, God's absolute power referred to his omnipotence pure and simple; it represented his own untrammelled nature and owed no obligation to sustain any fixed order. Ultimately, then, God in his absolute power was always able to override his ordinances, for the latter were only a specific application of his infinite power.

Now it would seem that the use of God's *potentia absoluta* was among the most potent forces in earlier fourteenth-century thought, and one which helped to transform traditional conceptions. While not in itself new—Peter Damian had invoked God's omnipotence in the eleventh century—its widespread application was. It reached its height during the decade of the 1340s at Paris, where the university authorities attempted to ban the doctrines to which it gave rise. But already in 1326 Ockham had had fifty-one articles taken from his writings and censured by a papal commission at Avignon, shortly before Eckhart's own articles were examined and condemned. Many of them show a striking similarity. In particular, one of their most important consequences was to dispense with intermediaries so far as God was concerned. God could do directly what he normally did through agents and could do so in his own way. Thus, among the articles for which Ockham was censured, were the statements that God could accept the act of free will of itself as meritorious without the need for prevenient grace (arts. 1–3); that sin can be remitted without grace (art. 4); that God can rightly be hated (arts. 5, 6); that the will in a state of grace could refuse blessedness (6, 46); the grace and sin do not exclude one another (87 and 8); that sin could be caused without sinning (9); that the vision of something can continue to exist after it has been destroyed (10); that man could only know naturally the proposition that God was the highest good without knowing that he was a Trinity (13) or anything concerning his essence (14, 15, 16, 17, 18); that the divine attributes and divine ideas could not be formally distinguished (25–30, 40, 41, 42, 44, 45); that the principle of something could be believed but the conclusion known (34); that Christ, as a man without grace, could sin (36); that the same body could be in several places at once (47) and several bodies in the same place at once (48). Together, it need hardly be said, these opinions constituted an attitude of uncertainty which made for the dissolution of accepted theological—and sometimes natural—landmarks. How far-reaching its effects were can be seen in the subsequent condemnations at Paris.

By the first, in 1340, the Rector of Paris university, John Buridan, condemned Ockhamism in general terms. It had engendered in the arts faculty an attitude of doubt towards the accepted authorities and towards the correspondence between terms and things, leading to conclusions that "Socrates and Plato, God and creatures, were nothing." The climax was reached in 1346 and 1347. In the former year the pope, in a letter to the masters and scholars of the university, attacked the recent tendency in both philosophy and theology to turn away from the accepted authorities to "new, strange and sophistical doctrines, said to be taught in certain other places of study, together with seemingly unreal and useless opinions which lead nowhere." The worst feature was disregard of the bible and the *sancti*, the very foundations of faith, in favour of "philosophical questions and other disputatious matters and suspect views." This letter, dated 20 May 1346, followed immediately on the condemnation of sixty articles taken from the writing of Nicholas of Autrecourt, on 19 May. When these are considered together with the condemnation of the fifty articles of John of Mirecourt in the following year, they give us some picture of the "pestiferous and pernicious" doctrines referred to in the pope's letter. Those of Nicholas were mainly concerned with the absence of natural certainty: that knowledge of the existence or non-existence of one thing does not enable us to deduce the existence or non-existence of another (1–8); that there is no certainty of natural substances or of causality (9–19); or of the greater nobility of one thing over another; or that God is "ens nobilissimum" (22); or that the expressions "God" and "creature" signify anything real (32, 54, 55). Finally, God could command a rational creature to hate him (58), and, if the former's will were dependent upon God, he could not sin or err (59). With John of Mirecourt, on the other hand, most of his opinions were concerned with moral theology, above all with God as the cause of sin (10–14, 16, 17, 18, 33, 34), of the soul's hate of him (31–32), and of all acts of the created will (35–38). John also repeated the current notions that Christ could mislead, be misled, and hate God (1–6); that God predestined on account of future good works and the proper use of free will (47–50); and that something higher than God could be envisaged (46).

PART V

Late Medieval Heresy and the Reformation

After the decline of Catharism in the thirteenth century, dissent of the Reformist variety again predominated. The Valdesian movement continued through the thirteenth century, although with diminishing strength. But later heresies of the thirteenth and fourteenth centuries, like the Speronists, Dolcinists, and *Apostolici*, were largely Reformist. The movements generated by the teachings of John Wyclif at the end of the fourteenth century—the Lollards in England and the Husites in Bohemia—were very much in the Reformist tradition. At the same time, they were close in spirit to the Protestant Reformation.

The degree of connection between late medieval heresy and the Reformation has long been debated. Traditional Protestant scholars affirmed that there was a direct connection, but this has been difficult to establish except in a vague sense. Some Protestants have maintained that though there may have been no specific historical tradition connecting the two, the work of the Holy Spirit in the minds of God's chosen vessels (heretical and Protestant) created the connection. But the historian, who is unable to examine the mind or to discern the policies of the Holy Spirit, is unable to accept this as an historical explanation. He may content himself with the observation that, whether or not there was any affiliation of Protestantism with medieval dissent, or whether the similarity arises out of similar though independent responses to similar though independent situations, the careers and attitudes of the Protestant Reformers resembled those of the medieval Reformists, with the chief difference that the political and social circumstances of the sixteenth century were much more conducive to a broad upheaval.

21   *Gordon Leff*
          Heresy and the Decline of the Medieval Church

Gordon Leff discusses the problem in an article by this title in Past and Present,
No. 20 (1961).

HERESY AND THE DECLINE OF THE MEDIEVAL CHURCH

The growth of heresy and the decline of the church from the later
thirteenth century are coming increasingly to be recognized as an
institutional rather than a spiritual phenomenon. There is a growing
realization that worldliness and wealth do not in themselves mark the
difference between the church in the twelfth and thirteenth centuries
and in the fourteenth and fifteenth centuries; what took place was not
a wholesale degeneration in either morals or personnel, but rather a
gradual revulsion against the church as the medium of spiritual and
intellectual life. Whereas the earlier period was predominantly one of
religious fervour under the aegis of the church, the later middle ages
witnessed an evergrowing series of extra-ecclesiastical movements,
indifferent or hostile to it. The difference was less one of spirituality
than of ecumenicality: between the ability to canalize the main
religious currents and alienation from them. Ultimately it became the
difference between ecclesiastical reform and ecclesiastical repression;
and it is this shift in emphasis which signalizes the changed state of the
church.

In looking at its causes it is as well to begin by eliminating past mis-
conceptions. Primary among them is the deep-seated belief that the
church became corrupt—politically, financially and in personnel—
and the mere vehicle for privilege and private aggrandisement; and
consequently that heresy was simply a rebellion against ecclesiastical
degeneration or a reaction to ecclesiastical oppression. Such a view,
implicit in many modern diagnoses, does not stand up to examination.
Firstly, it suffers from circularity in making moral decline the cause

SOURCE. Gordon Leff, "Heresy and the Decline of the Medieval Church," in *Past and
Present* (No. 20, April 1961), pp. 36–51. Reprinted by permission of *Past and Present
Society*, Corpus Christi College, Oxford and the author.

of moral decline: and even if it were granted, it would offer no explanation of why and how the decline happened in the first place. Secondly, it is manifestly untrue in a number of respects. To begin with, it represents a confusion between the papacy at one particular epoch and the church as a whole throughout the later middle ages. Leaving aside the abuses of the pontificates of Innocent IV, Urban IV and Boniface VIII during the middle and later thirteenth century in their struggle to gain control of Sicily, there is little or nothing that can justly be described as spiritually degenerate about the later papacy. If few popes were of the calibre of Gregory VII or Innocent III, equally few were of the stamp of these Sicilian popes. For the most part the Avigonese pontiffs were neither outstandingly good nor irredeemably bad; certainly not tyrants or mere extortioners. John XXII was overbearing but so had been Innocent III; Clement VI was given to splendour but it cannot be called corruption.

The case is similar in the papacy's relations with individual churches, especially over papal provisions. The latter were for long regarded as the most flagrant of all the abuses in the church: and as the epitome of papal self-seeking and the furtherance of papal interests for finacial gain at the expense of the ordinary indigenous clergy. It is true that under Innocent IV the practice did become a financial scandal; but any procedure can be distorted. In reality, however, it merely meant selecting a candidate for a vacancy centrally with papal approval instead of locally; and there is strong evidence to suggest that it was initiated not by the papacy but by pressure from below for a method of arbitrament among rival claimants. On theoretical grounds it could be upheld as aiding the best candidate as opposed to a favourite son. In practice, there is nothing to show that it normally represented more than the Pope formally assenting to an appointment to a benefice, usually from a number of applicants: that is to say, it was primarily a matter of procedure reflecting, at most, one aspect of the centralization common to all institutions in the high middle ages. Thus in England during the fourteenth century, although the appointment of bishops was by papal provision, the presence of aliens in English bishoprics and parishes was virtually unknown; and there is nothing to show that the king did not usually get his way over elections. Only in cathedral chapters was there a strong alien influx, but this hardly constituted the subservience of the English church to the papacy.

Finally, it should be remembered that during the fourteenth century the papacy, in common with the church generally, became less rather than more powerful. Where a fiat from Innocent III could throw the strongest monarch into disarray, the attempts at papal direction of secular powers were virtually spent with the defeat of Boniface VIII by Philip le Bel in 1303. This can be seen in the growing inability of the papacy to exercise direct control over individual churches, with a corresponding increase in direct secular control. Secular control had long existed *de facto*, but during the fourteenth century it became established as a matter of right. Not only did it entail the prohibition of clerical taxation without royal assent; it led to a direct attack on the prerogatives of the papacy, making the clergy of the state in question directly subject to royal demands. Thus Edward II, the weakest of fourteenth-century English kings, took £255,000 in taxation from the English church. There were also unprecedented assaults upon ecclesiastical property, as in Philip le Bel's suppression of the Templars, to say nothing of the anti-papal legislation of the Statutes of Provisors and Praemunire in England in 1351, 1353, and 1365.

For much of the fourteenth and fifteenth centuries the papacy was beset with growing troubles both internal and external. Internally, its exile to Avignon in 1305 reduced its freedom of movement: its lodgement on French soil and a succession of French popes gave it inevitably a more restricted character. The whole tradition of papal authority had sprung from its Petrine origin in Rome; *urbi* and *orbis* could not be separated with impunity. Then in the last quarter of the fourteenth century came the Great Schism which sapped it of any ecumenical effectiveness for forty years, at the very time of the great religious outbursts of Wyclif and Hus. Externally, the whole trend of development in the later middle ages militated against papal hegemony. Politically its traditional prerogatives were being eclipsed by the exigencies of the Hundred Years War, with heavier clerical taxation and increased hostility to papal intervention; in England in particular the Avignonese popes were under suspicion of French sympathies, and offers of mediation were never of permanent effect. Economically, socially, intellectually and spiritually, there was growing unrest, punctuated by widespread outbursts of anti-sacerdotalism—such as by the Lollards and the Hussites—as well as the great increase in both heretical and unorthodox religious movements. These put the papacy on the defensive and rendered its traditional position and prerogatives anachronistic.

In these different ways the papacy was shorn of its earlier authority and, above all, of its ecumenicality. The circumstances of its own development and of society at large led to the loss of its position as the spiritual and intellectual arbiter of christendom. It was here, and not merely in its spiritual life, that its real decline lay.

Similarly with the church as a whole, the waning of its influence was not primarily a spiritual matter, certainly not one of moral degeneration. As with the papacy, there is no evidence that as a general rule the clergy was more corrupt and less religious in the one hundred and fifty years after the death of Innocent III than in the same period before. We have only to turn to the leading English ecclesiastics of the thirteenth and fourteenth centuries: men like Grosseteste, Kilwardby, Peckham, Winchelsey, Lutteral, Bradwardine, Grandisson, Fitzralph are equal in stature to those of any comparable previous period, whilst the bishops of the later fourteenth century abound as founders of colleges and in the furtherance of learning. Indeed it can be said unequivocably that the standards of literacy and scholarship increased progressively from the thirteenth century onwards, primarily through the emergence of the universities as the virtually indispensable education for higher ecclesiatics. Of seventy-eight English bishops between 1215 and 1275, forty seem to have been *magistri* or university graduates, and in the reign of Edward II twenty-nine of forty-five bishops are known to have been graduates. Nor is it without significance that Winchelsey, the upright Archbishop of Canterbury, quashed the election of the Prior of Ely in 1302 because he had "insufficient literature"; or that a clerk of the Black Prince, Robert Stretton, a candidate for the see of Lichfield, was examined and failed three times, before being finally consecrated in 1360. The good were naturally balanced by the not so good and sometimes by the bad, but, taken as a whole, the higher ecclesiastics were at least as competent and learned as at any time in the middle ages.

Much the same could be said of the clergy generally. Pluralism and non-residence were endemic in a system in which preferment was treated as a reward from the hands of a doner, whether king, monastery, lay lord or pope. But if anything, the practice of papal provision acted as check on it. Even while reserving to themselves appointment to the higher cathedral offices, the popes of Avignon nevertheless attempted to restrict and control pluralism, notably by the three constitutions of Clement V, John XXII and Urban V. Nor was pluralism always excessive: the returns of pluralists (1366) in the dioceses of Salisbury and Norwich, for example, show that each pluralist held on average two or three benefices representing an aggregate income ranging from about £26 (Salisbury) to £30 (Norwich), hardly even at that time a fortune.

It is not the absence of shortcomings in the later medieval church, but their continuity with those of the earlier middle ages that deserves emphasis. Personal unfittedness, favoritism, abuse of position, greed and injustice were common to both epochs; they cannot be made the exclusive feature of the later church or a sign of a moral decline. The failings of the medieval church were inherent in it. While some—particularly those concerned with finance—became more pronounced, others—notably the degree of literacy and suitability of individual churchmen—became less so; neither way can they be regarded as of fundamental significance, distinguishing a morally sound from a corrupt body.

If we are to discover the causes of the church's loss of position we must look beyond the church itself to its role in society. In doing so, the question is no longer a moral one—whether the church as such was better or worse—but an institutional one of why it was unable to retain its spiritual and intellectual authority. Accordingly its success or failure is not to be measured by the degree to which it deviated from some ideal norm, but rather by its capacity to satisfy the demands that confronted it as an institution.

Now the first thing to be observed about heresy and opposition to the church in the later middle ages is that in themselves they were not new. From the later eleventh century onwards, in particular, there had been a steady stream of religious movements which, in varying degrees, represented a challenge to the authority of the church by acting outside its communion. The Waldensians, the Patarines, the Cathars, whatever their differences in outlook and origin, all came to be marked off from the main body of believers by their renunciation of the church's mediation. In doing so, they constituted a challenge to it, which, if allowed to pass unanswered, would have meant the loss of its ecumenicality and its authority.

Secondly, it is important to stress the nature of the challenge. It was not primarily an attack on the church but a withdrawal from it; it was impelled not so much by anti-sacerdotalism, and certainly not by a hostility to Christian belief, as by the desire to return to the practices of Christ and his apostles. Accordingly, as we shall see, the opposition to the church was secondary to the search for a new mode of spiritual life; and it was frequently the hostility of the Church—as with the Waldensians and Spiritual Franciscans—which caused such movements to become heretical. Nowhere is this so true as during the later middle ages, which, under the influence of M. Lagarde, have come to be regarded as the period of the emergence of the "lay spirit". In a certain sense, of course, it is true that there was a growing advocacy both in political theory and practice of the rights of the state at the expense of the church; also that intellectually the growing demarcation of faith from practical experience lent the latter greater autonomy and helped to foster the renewal of something akin to an attitude of empiricism in the fourteenth century. But except in its more directly political aspects, as in the policies of Philip le Bel of France or the writings of Marsilius of Padua, we cannot describe as "lay" the great majority of the anti- or extra-ecclesiastical movements of the time or the prevailing intellectual outlook. Indeed, the starting point in any examination of the religious discontent in the later middle ages must be to come to terms with its marked religious fervor. It was not merely an age disturbance; it was an age of *religious* disturbance, fed not by unbelief but by an excess of belief. Laicism, important as it may have been in certain respects, was never more than a by-product.

This is confirmed as soon as we consider the position of the church from say 1300 onwards. What we see is not the absence of piety but its increasing identification with heterodoxy. Where in earlier centuries the church had been able to canalize and institutionalize each main wave of religious fervor, first with the monasticism of Cluny, then Cîteaux and finally with the mendicant orders, it was henceforth unwilling and unable to do so. Spiritual—and with it intellectual—reform now largely lay outside the control of the church; the unofficial believer, rich or humble, supplanted the priest, the monk and the friar as the vehicle of religious fervor. It was the scale and multiplicity of this change which constituted the difference between the state of the church in 1200 and 1300. Where previously heterodoxy had been localized in certain regions—as with the Albigensians in Languedoc—and certain social strata—such as the poor men of Lyons (the Waldensians) and the Patarines in Lombardy—it now became so widespread as to be universal; it erupted not only in new movements like the Béguines and Béghards, and the Brethren of the Free Spirit as well as taking root in the Franciscan order, but in a new outlook—mysticism. Together they gave expression to the two great cries which had long been the hallmark of reform no less than of heresy: poverty, or at least austerity of life, and direct experience of God. Both, and especially the second, could take a number of forms, and so long as the successive reforming movements had been assimilated to the church there had been only a residual challenge from those who upheld these beliefs. But once they were able to go unchecked they became a direct threat to its very foundations. Poverty, the renunciation of all possessions on the model of Christ and his disciples, was physically incompatible with the existence of the church as a corporation; its entire structure rested upon its endowments, taxation, tithes and the continuity by which its authority was maintained. These had come to be enshrined in the privileges and immunities which it enjoyed; without them it would have been nothing as the reforming popes of the eleventh century realized in their struggle against lay control. Direct personal experience of God and its propagation through preaching, unless adapted to the sacramental life of the church, constituted an even greater threat; for, carried to its conclusion, it meant nothing less than entirely renouncing the arbitrament of the church and denying its *raison d'être* as the expression of God's saving will on earth.

The convergence of these two attitudes was the thread which ran alike through heresy and religious reform; but it was from the later thirteenth century onwards that they became a danger of the first magnitude and one which the church could only meet by repression rather than example. More than anything else it was its inability to maintain its spiritual hegemony, and its increasing dependence upon the Inquisition to combat rather than initiate reform, that helped to turn into heresy what in the eleventh and twelfth centuries would have been legitimized within the church. Here above all lay the testimony to its decline: in the passing of spiritual fervor to movements beyond its control. The effect was to accentuate still further the division between orthodoxy and heterodoxy. On the one hand, any group however small or however quietist, came to be treated as potentially heretical. On the other, this inflexibility of attitude helped to drive men to look outside the church for spiritual values.

The consequences of this *impasse* are nowhere more apparent than in the history of the Spiritual Franciscans, the Zealots. They provide the outstanding example of piety turning, or better being turned, into heresy. The Spirituals originated from that part of the order which desired to hold fast to their founder's conception of Christianity modelled upon the mendicant poverty of Christ and his disciples. They regarded the wealth and organization inseparable from the institutionalization of the Franciscans as one of the two leading orders of Friars, as in conflict with first principles. Stimulated by the writings of Joachim of Flora (1145–1202), Abbot of St. John, Calabria—who foresaw the coming, after the destruction of the present age, of a new and third age, the era of the Holy Spirit, to be preached by "an order of bare-footed monks"—they denounced the holding of all wealth and property. The conviction with which they held to their ideal led them into growing opposition to the official wing of the order and the papacy, and to the fall in 1257 of the Franciscan General, John of Parma, for his sympathies with the Spirituals. The latter rebelled against the legal compromise established in 1229 by Pope Gregory IX whereby all the property in the hands of the order belonged to the Church. Instead they demanded a life of actual, not legal, poverty, a doctrine that came to be known as the *usus pauper*. As the wealth and luxury of life of the order continued to increase so did the hostility of the Zealots towards it, culminating in the struggle over the doctrine of the Poverty of Christ.

This dispute, over whether Christ's poverty was a dogma of the church, marked what might be called the final parting of the ways. That the actual occasion for it was the arrest by the Inquisition at Narbonne of a certain Béguin for spreading the doctrine is indicative of how far it had become identified with subversion. The remarkable series of pamphlets to which it gave rise showed how fundamental the issue was. The Pope, John XXII, the most masterful of all the Avignonese popes, in his Bull "Ad conditorem canonum" followed the doctrine which had already been enunciated by Aquinas, that charity not poverty was the basis of the perfect life; and he went on to cut the ground from under the Franciscans' feet by denying the distinction between use and possession, thereby implicating the order in the practice of the whole church. Although he subsequently modified this, the whole doctrine of poverty was declared anathema in the Bull "Cum inter nonnullos" in 1323. The Franciscan order was split. Those who continued to champion poverty became known as the *Fraticelli* and divided into two groups: the direct successors of the older Spirituals living a life of holiness and poverty, mainly in the cities of Italy; and the Michaelists, the followers of Michael Cesena, General of the Franciscans at the time of the dispute, who conformed more to the model of the Church and whose center was the March of Ancona. But the influence of the Spirituals did not stop there; the so-called Béguines of Southern France, mainly in Narbonne, Toulouse and Provence, as well as in Catalonia, seem to have adopted many of their ideals with especial emphasis upon mendicancy, manual labor and Christ's Poverty. Indeed the very term Béguine, as that of *Fraticelli*, was employed by the ecclesiastical authorities as a term of abuse; in reality there was little to point to a genuine connection between the sects in Southern France and their Northern namesakes.

The Franciscan Spirituals were only one of a great number of such movements; what distinguished them was that their struggle took place within the very heart of the church. As Grundmann has shown, these movements were not confined to any one stratum of society, or indeed to any region. Nor did they have any coherent program. While they were often influenced by an apocalyptic vision as with the Joachists, some of the Flagellants and that mysterious body the Brethren of the Free Spirit, they did not in general constitute a revolutionary force for the overthrow of the existing order. Rather, from the later twelfth century onwards, they became what might be called a growing non-conformist element existing alongside the church; as such they formed a permanent part of the landscape for the rest of the middle ages, a presence with which the church had to reckon and which it attempted to combat. While all these movements practised poverty and austerity of life they were by no means drawn from the poor: the Albigensians, who came nearest to presenting a full-fledged alternative to the life of the church, owed their strength to support from the aristocracy of Southern France; the Béguines were in origin an aristocratic movement drawn from devout women; the Rhineland mystics associated with the Brethren of the Free Spirit, were certainly not unlettered poor men; and the Spiritual Franciscans included some of the most eminent men of the order, such as Hugh of Digne, John of Parma, Peter John Olivi, Michael of Cesena and in a metaphorical sense St. Francis himself. The same can be said of the later movements inspired by Wyclif and Hus. Just as the church was a mirror of society, sharing its extremes of rank, wealth, life and intellectual opportunities, so were the movements which grew up outside it. Not only were they frequently inspired by men and doctrines orthodox in origin, but they embraced whole regions rather than existing as specific groups: the Albigensians and the Waldensians in Southern France and Italy, the Béguines in the Low Countries and perhaps Southern France, the mystics in the Rhineland and Holland, the Lollards in England, the Hussites in Bohemia. While they overlapped and varied in the sources of their strength—e.g. towns or countryside—they tended to dominate a whole area as the constant operations of the Inquisition abundantly testify.

There were similar developments in the intellectual life of the later middle ages. The later thirteenth and the fourteenth centuries were punctuated by a series of condemnations first of Aristotelianism and then of Ockhamism. The change was a significant one. Where the former more than anything else offered a direct challenge to the Christian belief by denying its main tenets of the creation, the Incarnation, an individual soul and so on, Ockhamism came nearer to presenting an alternative Christian interpretation. Together with the mysticism which came from the Rhineland, through the translations of Proclus and Plotinus, it offered the main doctrinal challenge of the fourteenth century. Different though the two were, they united in positing a rival to the existing dispensation; each put the emphasis upon God's direct intervention: the Ockhamists by stressing his ability to by-pass all secondary causes even should it mean God's contravening his own decrees; the mystics like Eckhart, Tauler, Suso and Ruysbruck by positing an immediate contact with God in the soul. While the one dominated the intellectual life, certainly of Northern Europe, the other became the foremost spiritual force of the fourteenth and fifteenth centuries. It was associated with every movement, orthodox as well as heterodox; it embraced the Dominicans—Eckhart, Tauler, Suso—as well as the Franciscans and the *Fraticelli*; it informed the Brethren of the Common Life as well as the Brethren of the Free Spirit; it produced great mystics in every country, Catherine of Siena in Italy, Ruysbruck in the Netherlands, the English mystics Julian of Norwich, Richard Rolle, Walter Hilton to mention only a few. Above all, in the growth of the "New Devotion" in the Netherlands in the later fourteenth and fifteenth centuries it led directly on to the final breach with the hierarchy of the Roman church.

In all these cases, whether within the communion of the church or outside it, the search for new forms of religious life and experience marked a rejection of the sacramental life of the church. Whatever form it might take, whether inspiring the ecstasies of the Flagellants, whose self-chastisement replaced the symbolism of the mass, or the quietism of the Brethren of the Common Life founded by Gerard de Groote, the traditional authority of the church was denied.

Now in seeking the explanation of these developments there are two distinct considerations. The first is the position of the church as the spiritual and intellectual arbiter of Christendom. As the one communion for all believers, it was confronted at any time with the problem of how to remain spiritually comprehensive and yet institutionally effective: that is to say, of how to meet developments in religious and intellectual life without impairing its authority or its principles. So long, as during the earlier middle ages, as there had been no serious rivals to the church's supremacy, the problem had not arisen; for the church had then constituted the sole cohesive and unifying body in society, the repository of all knowledge and spirituality, indispensable alike to the strongest ruler and the humblest believer. Its strength derived from the very lack of a settled order in which its own needs for reform and peace expressed the aspirations of society in general. Under the successive monastic and papal reforming movements, the church in the tenth, eleventh and twelfth centuries was itself the source of the fervor which marked the religious and intellectual life of the period. It led those very forces of opposition to luxury and oppression which later it repressed; its crusading zeal was against the infidel rather than the erring believer.

But the very success of the church was one of the main causes of its subsequent loss of position. In the first place it grew in wealth and privilege: endowment, the establishment of a system of taxation ordinary and extraordinary, its comprehensive tariff of fees extending from birth to death, and perhaps above all the prosperity of the monastic orders, particularly the Cistercians, made the church the wealthiest body in christendom. Inevitably, quite apart from the effects upon its way of life, it meant a change in outlook; it became a major preoccupation to safeguard its rights and dues as a corporation. Throughout the thirteenth century and beyond there was at all levels a constant outcry against ecclesiastical exactions. Innocent III's letters abound in complaints about clerical abuses and he pointed the contrast between the laxity of the clergy of the Midi and the austerity of the heretical Albigensian *perfecti*. With Innocent IV, half a century later, the Pope was himself among the most culpable; and although he was exceptional, the reputation of the church, and certainly of the papacy, suffered from its association with extortion. English chroniclers from Matthew Paris to Adam Murimuth set up a chorus of denunciation of the curia's exactions. At the same time, the triumph of the policies of the church reformers of the eleventh and twelfth centuries had firmly established the privileges of the church: not only was it a corporation in its own right, virtually immune from lay jurisdictions as the struggle between Henry II of England and Becket had shown; it also had the power to make and unmake the highest or the lowest in Christendom as Innocent III's pontificate so amply demonstrated. As its own position as the spiritual and intellectual arbiter of society became increasingly defined, through practice and canon law, the distinction between orthodoxy and heresy became ever more clearcut. The enactments of the Third (1179) and Fourth (1215) Lateran Councils in particular showed how important the question of opposition was becoming. In the words of Innocent III: "We consider that it is necessary to regard as manifest heretics those who preach or profess public ideas contrary to the Catholic faith and defend error.

In this sense, then, it is not untrue to say that the church helped to make heretics by insistence upon its prerogatives. It presented itself as one more priviledged body, both as landlord and as keeper of men's souls and minds. It was this combination which made it so vulnerable to opposition; for one tended to undermine the other. To demand tithes, taxes for crusades, and to enforce customary dues upon tenants, was to appear much as any lay landlord; on the other hand, of its nature the church claimed to speak for every sort and condition of men. In one sense it did; but in order to make its voice more effective it took on those very attributes of wealth and exclusiveness that removed it from the lower orders. Accordingly it became less able not merely to preach austerity and primitive simplicity, but to allow their practice either within its ranks or by laymen. The successive evolution of each religious movement to wealth and privilege meant one less bond with the poor and humble. Cluny and then Cîteaux, the main sources of religious fervor from the tenth to the twelfth centuries, each took its place in the hierarchy, the Cistercians through their custom of living separately from the secular world often causing villages to be depopulated on lands made over to them. The same corporate aspect of the church was to be seen in the intransigence with which, despite the amenability of individual churchmen, it opposed the demands of self-government among the communes during the eleventh and twelfth centuries wherever its own rights were concerned. Not surprisingly, therefore, the church became part of the established hierarchy of society. Its own structure was correspondingly hierarchichal, in the division between the princes of the church and the lower clergy. The former, drawn most often either from royal ministers or the nobility, lived the life of great lords, even unruly ones; the lower clergy, on the other hand, were frequently indistinguishable from the ordinary peasantry, either in their way of life or attainments. Pluralism and the practice of benefice-holders installing vicars as deputies while themselves taking the profits, meant the meanest conditions for many parish priests. They constituted a potent source of resentment, as the sermon literature of the later middle ages shows.

The second feature of the decline in the church is to be found in the development of society, mainly in the later part of the twelfth century. Firstly, there was the growth of urban centers, primarily in Lombardy and Flanders but also generally throughout Europe.

This led not simply to concentrations of population. It also meant—particularly in the industrial textile cities—new social groups, often verging on a proletariat, which had no sympathy with the increasing exclusiveness of the church and the structure of the monastery. They represented a different experience and a different outlook; their emphasis, as with the Waldensians, Albigensians, Patarines, upon austerity and the unfittedness of wordlings to hold spiritual authority flew directly in the face of the church. Secondly, and inseparable from this, was the influence of the East, above all doctrinally. From the first third of the twelfth century there was an influx of new ideas from the Moslem world. These were of two main kinds: renewed knowledge of Aristotle and some Greek science, together with the discovery of Islamic thought; and contact with heresies, the most potent of which was Catharism or Manichaeism. Both kinds constituted a challenge to Christian teaching and to both the church offered resistance; but whereas much of the former could be and was adjusted to and in some degree incorporated into a Catholic framework, the latter was an outright challenge which had to be rejected. The result was that, to the simple desire to lead a Christian life on the model of Christ and his disciples, was added a complex of beliefs the effect of which was to set up a rival outlook to that of the church, and to give heresy an intellectual backing which was of crucial importance in its growth in the thirteenth and fourteenth centuries. In addition to the overtly subversive and non-Christian doctrines, of which Catharism was the outstanding example, there were distortions of traditional doctrines. Of these, pantheism, associated with the Amaurians, Averroism and mysticism were the dominant offshoots. While the first two were more directly unchristian, it was mysticism deriving from the translations of Proclus, Plotinus and the pseudo-Dionysius in the thirteenth century, which came to constitute the main stream of unorthodoxy. With its emphasis upon inner experience of God through contemplation, it gave fullest expression to the rejection of the mediation of the church and the priesthood, whether through the quietism of Ruysbruck and the Flemish and Rhineland mystics or the more ecstatic attitudes of the Flagellants and the Brethren of the Free Spirit. The very presence of non-Christian ideas broke the intellectual monopoly which the church had previously enjoyed. The universities were never to the same degree ecclesiastically directed as the earlier cathedral schools had been; the growth of a professional class of teachers who had never gone beyond the study of the Arts—predominantly the works of Aristotle—meant that profane knowledge came to exist in its own right, untutored by theology. The conflict between the two became one of the dominant intellectual themes of the middle and early thirteenth century culminating in the condemnations of pagan, Aristotelian and Arabic concepts at the universities of Paris and Oxford in 1277. Henceforth reason was less and less harnessed to faith; and with the weakening of the bonds between them, each went increasingly its own way, often with extreme results as shown in the doctrine of Ockhamism and the condemnations of those associated with it at Paris in the 1340s.

This intellectual ferment was stimulated by the growth of preaching, popularized largely by the mendicant orders. Its impact in an age where the pulpit was the only means of communication need hardly be stressed. It is enough to draw attention to the denunciatory temper of so much sermon literature; the emphasis upon the vices and short-comings of the church was universal, and shows that the strictures of Wyclif, Langland and Chaucer were no isolated expressions, but part of the general atmosphere of criticism directed from below at the entire structure of the church.

Thirdly, the position of the church suffered from the growth of secular power, not only in the ways already mentioned, but in the loss of initiative entailed. Foremost was the decline of the crusading ideal. The heyday of papal supremacy had largely coincided with the comparative immaturity of secular kingdoms. Thus it had been able to unite support for the crusade under its leadership. The failure of the third crusade marked the end of this phase; it received its final death-knell with the fiasco of the fourth crusade which ended with the sack of Constantinople in 1204. Henceforth individual states were too strongly entrenched: and the papacy, for all its attempts, was never able to transcend its own involvements in secular politics; both its voice and with it its prestige were lost in the struggle for Italy and Sicily.

The consequence of these developments was that the church was forced on to the defensive; its area of control was narrowed; universality became incompatible with the preservation of its prerogatives: either it had to surrender its religious and intellectual monopoly or it had to oppose the threats to it. The turning point came with the Albigensian crusade; the invocation of force by Innocent III meant the failure to cope with heresy except by repression. The whole of the church was implicated: the older monastic orders as well as the new order of what was to be the Dominican Friars, the local clergy as well as the greatest pope of the middle ages. Insensibly it

meant a reorientation in the entire position of the church. To begin
with the church was now aligned with the lay power in opposing
further reform. The calling-in of the Northern French nobles to ex-
tirpate the heretics of Languedoc set in motion the process that within
a short span of time culminated in the Inquisition. A few years later in
1215 the Fourth Lateran Council sanctioned pastoral inquiries and the
abandonment of the heretic to the secular authority. In 1231 came the
legislation of Gregory X under which the procedures of the Inquisition
were established: the heretic having been excommunicated was to be
handed over to the secular judge for burning; all adherents of
the Cathars, Waldensians, Patarines and other heretics and anyone
communing with them, were excommunicated. Lay powers co-
operated in these actions, notably Frederick II and St. Louis who
offered a reward of one mark for every heretic captured. Nothing
could have been better calculated to drive heretics further away from
the church than its open hostility to them and its reliance upon
coercion. Although the intensity of repression varied from time to
time and place to place, it represented the refusal or inability to
countenance new forms of belief and therefore further religious
movements. This was specifically stated at the Fourth Lateran council,
in which the thirteenth canon formally forbade the foundations of
new orders and enjoined those who wished to take up monastic life
to enter one of the existing orders. For a time even the Dominicans
had to choose an established rule, that of the Augustinian canons.

Although the new mendicant orders of the Franciscans,
Dominicans, Carmelites and Augustinians all came into being at or
after this very time when new ones were being forbidden, they
marked the high-tide of religious expansion; as they gradually lost
impetus towards the end of the thirteenth century, there was nothing
to replace them. The whole direction of the policy of the church was
to prevent the spread of unorthodoxy. This had its effect upon the new
orders themselves. They became the main bulwarks of orthodoxy,
both spiritually and intellectually. The Dominicans had originated
in attempts to convert the heretics of the Midi: they largely operated
the Inquisition; and in the universities, despite the bitter strife with
the seculars at Paris, it was the Franciscan and Dominican thinkers
who succeeded in christianizing Aristotle.

As a result the church not only froze in its own positions; it tried
to halt any form of non-ecclesiastical development, looking askance,
as we have seen, on all attempts to pursue a life of simplicity and
austerity. The point hardly needs laboring that such a task was

impossible, not least because this repressive attitude engendered the very consequences it sought to avoid, by compelling men to look outside the church for spiritual fulfillment. At the same time, in the growing social unrest which marked the later middle ages, the church became the main object of hostility as epitomizing both material privilege and spiritual and intellectual autocracy. It was inevitably in the forefront of the whole breakdown of the medieval order and the waning of hierarchy.

It can be said, therefore, that the decline of the medieval Church was more than a mere matter of spiritual corruption on its part or of the growth of a lay spirit in opposition to it. Its cause is to be found in an evolution of both church and society, which undermined the ecumenical position of the church as the spiritual and intellectual arbiter of Europe. The conflict to which it gave rise was due as much to the church's attempt to retain this position as to the opposition to it. Ultimately the heresies and heterodox doctrines which arose were less the result of good versus evil, than of a turning away from an institution which of its nature could not both abide by the present order and assimilate the future.

22   *John Wyclif*

a. Wyclif's Career. *Wyclif's career and influence are discussed here by K. B. McFarlane, author of* The Origins of Religious Dissent in England.

WYCLIFFE AND OXFORD

When he died on 31 December 1384 John Wycliffe was about fifty-five years of age. By contemporary standards therefore he was a moderately old man. Yet until its last decade his life, though it had brought him distinction of a modest sort among his fellow-scholars, had been quite unremarkable and save for what was to follow would

SOURCE. K. B. McFarlane, *The Origins of Religious Dissent in England* (London: The English Universities Press Limited, 1966); originally published as *John Wycliffe and the Beginnings of English Nonconformity* (New York: Crowell-Collier & Macmillan, Inc., 1952), pp. 17–18, 199–201. Reprinted by permission of the publisher.

have attracted little posthumous notice. Had his death occurred in 1374 or even as much as a year or two later Wycliffe would be remembered only by specialist historians as one of the lesser ornaments of medieval Oxford. They would know him as the author of a number of philosophical works of no particular brilliance though of sustained competence, several of which, despite his enormous reputation, have not yet been found worthy of print. To the common reader he would be no more familiar than are those two precursors to whom he was most indebted, Bradwardine and FitzRalph, which is as much as to say not at all. It was only when this middle-aged doctor of divinity abandoned his crowded lecture-room for the royal service that there began that period of frenzied agitation upon which his later fame depends.

Even then it was not at once apparent that anything abnormal was to be expected. For a successful theologian to seek more profitable employment for his talents in the king's pay was usual enough. It was only when he decided, some eight years at most before his death, to propagate his unorthodox views among the ill-educated laity that Wycliffe's progress became definitely eccentric. From the very nature of their speculations medieval scholars were apt to fall into heresy, but the range of their influence did not ordinarily extend beyond the walls of the universities in which they taught; their profundities were too deep to be plumbed by any but their academic equals and the last thing they desired was a popular following. It was the extra-mural character of Wycliffe's appeal that gave it its marked singularity. He came to be the revered leader of men who could neither grasp his reasoning nor even, indeed, understand that Latin language in which it was normally expressed. It was for this betrayal of his order that he was most bitterly denounced by his academic opponents. His first disciples were learned popularisers; they invited the common man to spurn his official pastors and to teach himself heresy; and to help him in the work they translated the Bible and composed simple vernacular statements of their faith. They were different from the other clerical agitators with which the fourteenth century abounded, in that they were university-trained members of an intellectual *élite*; moreover, their leader was generally recognized to be the most outstanding scholar of his day. That such men should inspire and foster a heretical movement among the lesser clergy and the laity was rather as if a group of barons had stirred up a peasants' revolt.

EPILOGUE

Doctrinaire intellectuals in politics are rarely formidable for long. When Wycliffe died most of the causes for which he fought so vigorously had been lost, thanks largely to his complete indifference to political strategy. His evolution from schoolman into heretic, at least in its later stages, was as unexpected as it was unwelcome to his aristocratic employers. They were soon doing their best to silence him and to nullify his work. Their success makes it easier to admire his zeal than to forgive him his lack of worldly wisdom.

His catastrophic incompetence as a practical reformer does not, however, in the least embarrass his modern admirers. Doctrinaires, for all the adversity and disillusionment that they suffer in their lives, have one consolation: they may enjoy long after death apotheosis at the hands of equally doctrinaire historians. So it has been with Wycliffe. Thanks to a Reformation he did little or nothing to inspire and in effect everything possible to delay, he has been hailed for centuries as its Morning Star, the herald of its dawn. Yet Wycliffe, in fact, did more than any man in Catholic England—though admittedly that was not his intention—to discredit even moderate reform with the political class which alone had the power to carry it out. As if the Henrician Reformation could have happened against the will of Henry VIII and the men of property! It was impossible without their active co-operation. The successes of Luther and Calvin were a tribute to the political anarchy where their work was done; in England, their shrift would have been as short as Wycliffe's.

Nothing is to be gained by over-estimating the extent of the English heresiarch's achievement. His excesses and, still more, those of his disciples made reform disreputable and prepared the way for the easy triumph of reaction. Lollardy had always appealed most strongly to the lower middle class; after 1414 that class monopolised it completely. That is why it had very little influence on the Reformation when it came. The establishment of a state church under the supreme headship of the king brought no end to the persecution of the Lollards. Their feeble protest was ultimately drowned in the louder chorus of protestant nonconformity. Their heirs were, in short, not the Anglicans, but the Brownists and the Independents.

This may have been far from their founder's original purpose. For Wycliffe had not very much in common with the weavers of Bristol and the butcher of Standon, whose opinions would perhaps have shocked him. But it was he who first taught them to question the church's sacramental system. He therefore set them on the road that could only lead them to death or an humiliating submission. Yet prot-estants of many shades from Bale, Foxe and Milton to such latterday writers as Trevelyan and Workman have agreed "to regard with thank-fulness and pride" a ministry so disastrous in its consequences.

It is not surprising that with this naïve approach to history they are also grossly unfair to the men on whom fell the duty of persecution. Credit is rarely given to the bishops for their conscientious efforts to induce their victims to submit or for their reluctance to see even the obstinate go to their deaths. Yet, apart from the loud-mouthed and bloodthirsty Despenser—whose actions in the case were less ruthless than his reported speech—there was no bishop who showed a delight in the sport. Both Courtenay and Arundel set their suffra-gans an example of scrupulous patience and restraint. Arundel's treatment of Purvey was particularly magnanimous. That a man should be burnt for a refusal to accept the church's teaching as author-itative, we may all now agree, is monstrous. But it was possible to think differently in 1401 whithout being a monster. Compared with most religious—and some political—persecutors, the bishops of fifteenth-century England were humane, hesitant, almost squeamish. That they have been depicted otherwise since the days of Foxe does not say as much for English historians. Indignation and pity for the martyrs can easily prevent us from doing impartial justice alike to persecutors and persecuted. It is more important to understand than to side instinctively with the under-dog.

Calamitous as were the efforts of Wycliffe as a practical reformer, his life and teaching yet deserve at least as much study as they have received. Whatever mistakes he made as a political strategist, he still remains one of the most remarkable figures of his age. His vitality and the fearlessness of his thought—the very qualities which interfered with his success in action—shine beneath the dust and tarnish of nearly six centuries. Time has reduced most of his great contempo-raries to vague, scarcely discernible shapes; Wycliffe, in spite of the enormous gaps in the evidence, lives, if as a force more than as a man. His career has besides a special value for the student of late medieval history. As a scholar, politician, preacher and rebel he touched his times at so many points that to follow him through his various avoca-tions is to learn much that is worth knowing about the England of his day. The Lollard sect may have been hopelessly outmatched, but the fortunes of its hunted and sometimes martyred apostles help us to a better understanding of the society which they strove in vain to alter.

For the historian, indeed, the reformation that did not come off is scarcely less interesting than the one that did.

    b. Wyclif's Beliefs. *John Wyclif expressed his beliefs in this dialogue, taken from* Tracts and Treatises of John de Wycliffe, D. D.

ALITHIA. We have here touched on the subject of indulgences; and as the granting of these appears to me quite in accordance with this blasphemous presumption of the friars, I could wish that you would say something on this topic.

PHRONESIS. As the pride of those who hate God ever tends upward, so although the fountain head of heresy and sin takes its rise in the very beginning of darkness, the rivulet of the friars strives unnaturally to raise itself above its source. I confess that the indulgences of the pope, if they are what they are said to be, are a manifest blasphemy, inasmuch as he claims a power to save men almost without limit, and not only to mitigate the penalties of those who have sinned, by granting them the aid of absolution and indulgences, that they may never come to purgatory, but to give command to the holy angels, that when the soul is separated from the body, they may carry it without delay to its everlasting rest.

The frairs give a color to this blasphemy, by saying that Christ is omnipotent, and excels all his good angels, and that the pope is his plenary vicar on earth, and so possesses in everything the same power as Chirst in his humanity. It is here that lawyers, in common with the friars, cry as wolves, and, contradicting themselves, say that when they consider the power of this God upon earth they cannot lift up their face to heaven. Whence, to declare the power of the pope, the false brethren, according to the secrets of their faith, proceed as follows:

They suppose, in the first place, that there is an infinite number of supererogatory merits, belonging to the saints, laid up in heaven, and above all, the merit of our Lord Jesus Christ, which would be sufficient to save an infinite number of other worlds, and that, over all this treasure, Christ hath set the pope. Secondly, that it is his pleasure to distribute it, and, accordingly, he may distribute therefrom to an infinite extent, since the remainder will still be infinite. Against this rude blasphemy I have elsewhere inveighed. Neither the pope nor

SOURCE. John Wycliffe. "Indulgences and Penance (Fourteenth Century)," in *Tracts and Treatises of John de Wycliffe, D.D.* (London: Blackburn and Pardon, 1845), pp. 174–180.

the Lord Jesus Christ can grant dispensations or give indulgences to any man, except as the Deity had eternally determined by his just counsel. But we are not taught to believe that the pope, or any other man, can have any color of justice to adduce for so doing; therefore, we are not taught that the pope has any such power. . . .

This doctrine is a manifold blasphemy against Christ, inasmuch as the pope is extolled above his humanity and deity, and so above all that is called God—pretensions which, according to the declarations of the apostle, agree with the character of Antichrist; for he possesses Caesarean power above Christ, who had not where to lay his head. In regard to spiritual power, so far as the humanity of Christ is concerned, it would seem that the pope is superior to our Lord Jesus Christ; for it behoved Christ to suffer the most bitter passion for the salvation of man; and we believe, that on the ground of the Divine justice, men attain to whatever happiness may be theirs by virtue of Christ's passion. But this renegade says, that it is allowable that he should live as luxuriously as he may choose, and that, by the bare writing of one of his scribes, he can introduce wonders, without limit, into the church militant! Who, then, can deny his being extolled above the Lord Jesus Christ, in whose life we read not that Christ, or any one of his apostles, granted such absolutions or indulgences? Yet, had such power been at their command, it is on many grounds probable that they would not have been absolutely idle in the use of it, especially when Christ condemns the slothful servant, for not trafficking with the talent entrusted to him; and he requires at the hand of the prelate the souls committed to his care, and lost through his negligence, as appears from the third chapter of Ezekiel. Which alternative, then, should we maintain, that Christ and his apostles possessed no such power, or that they were culpable in hoarding such treasure, in place of bringing it forth for the good of the church? But what greater insanity than to adopt such a conclusion!

Similar in its folly is the doctrine which teaches, that the pope dispenses those same merits of the saints, for the service of men, to any extent, according to his pleasure. For it behoves Christ to do more, both on his own part, to fulfil the claims of justice; and on that of the sinner, whom it becomes him to affect, imparting grace to him, that he may prove worthy of the Divine assistance.

The same may be said concerning the fiction of the keys of Antichrist, for it is not necessary that the believer should insist on the foundation of this pretension, since the argument will be found to be one without sequence. Christ, they say, granted to Peter, the apostle in the nearest degree following his own example, such power over the keys, and therefore we ought, in the same manner, to concede to Antichrist, who, in word and deed, is still more pre-eminently his opposite, as great, or even greater, power in the church! Christ gave to Peter, and to others possessing a knowledge of the law of God, power of judging according to the law of that knowledge, both in binding and loosing, agreeably to the church triumphant. But, now, this renegade will not be regulated by the mind of the church above, nor by any authority; but, as might be expected from Antichrist, he sets forth new laws, and insists, under pain of the heaviest censure, that the whole church militant shall believe in them; so that anything determined therein, shall stand as though it were a part of the Gospel of Jesus Christ.

In such infinite blasphemies is the infatuated church involved, especially by the means of the tail of this dragon—that is, the sects of the friars—who labor in the cause of this illusion, and of other Luciferian seductions of the church. But arise, O soldiers of Christ! be wise to fling away these things, along with the other fictions of the prince of darkness, and put ye on the Lord Jesus Christ, and confide, undoubtedly, in your own weapons, and sever from the church such frauds of Antichrist, and teach the people that in Christ alone, and in his law, and in his members, they should trust; that in so doing, they may be saved through his goodness, and learn above all things honestly to detect the devices of Antichrist!

ALITHIA. You would oblige me now by stating your views of the sacrament of penance. To define it seems difficult, for it is said that penitence hath three parts, like a harp, namely, contrition of heart, confession with the mouth, and satisfaction by deeds—and its genus, accordingly, is not easily specified, these three things being diverse in genus.

PHRONESIS. It appears to me that penitence consists in the condition of the mind, and that these other things, which are called the parts of penitence, are its accidents, which go together to form its completeness. Contrition belongs to the mind alone, and is not an object of sense, inasmuch as the contrite confess to the Lord. And this department of penitence, though little esteemed, is yet of the greatest virtue, so that without it the rest avail nothing. Confession is made up of this feeling, and of oral utterance made to God alone. And thus the fathers under the old law, in common with those of the New Testament, were accustomed to confess. Penitence, in the sense of satisfaction by works, is made up of the two former, together with a confession made to the priest in private.

Now from a regard to gain, it is to this last view of penitence that we give most attention. But whether this third kind is necessary to salvation, or on what authority it was introduced, is with many a matter of dispute. But we must confide on this point in John, who, in his gloss on the decrees, says, after stating many opinions which he censures, that Innocent III invented it, and to confirm it, established the law "Omnis utriusque sexus," which is set forth in the fifth decretal. But in my opinion, as I have explained at length, it would be better for the church did she content herself with the first and second kinds of penitence as above mentioned. But though the third form (confession to a priest) is injurious to many, and is the cause of many evils to both parties (the priest and the one confessing), nevertheless it brings many good results to the church, and since it might possibly be well conducted, it appears to me that it may be, by supposition, necessary, and so really necessary, forasmuch as many, through shame of being obliged to confess the sin, and of submitting to the penance enjoined, and from the fear of being obliged to make confession of what they have done elsewhere, are deterred from repeating their sin.

No one can believe that a man may not be saved without confession of this kind, for, otherwise, all the dead from Christ's ascension to the time of Innocent III are lost—a horrible thing to believe. Rather do we think, that a much greater number are lost under the law of that pope on this subject, than would ever have been lost for the want of it. Besides, it generally happens that he who absolves is not acquainted with the magnitude of the sin confessed, just as he knows not if the man who is confessing be contrite; though he is well aware that unless he be so, his sin is not removed. How, then, can he utter falsehoods in the name of Christ, and so impudently absolve sin, and enjoin a penance which he cannot know as being proportioned to the transgression? Neither is it lawful to burden the church with new traditions, especially such as are of a suspicious character, for what we have is already sufficient. And the laws about confession in the Scripture have served us well enough for more than a thousand years. On what ground, then, is it that without a law a third kind of penitence has been introduced in a manner so unlikely? It appears to me, that this papal law is to be admitted as far as the discretion of the person who confesses may deem profitable.

ALITHIA. I see, brother, that you allow but little weight to this papal law; and it seems to me, that for the same reason, you would make light of the absolution from penalty and guilt, and the full remission of sin granted by the pope, and of that burden of sin which the prelate often aggravates by fulminating his horrible excommunications, and so the decision of the court of Rome, on such matters, would fall to the ground.

PHRONESIS. The observations you make seem to involve much truth, inasmuch as in the Scriptures, without any additions on the part of the Roman court, it is sufficiently set forth how every man should regulate his life. And if the injunctions of Scripture are attended to, it follows that the man who lives to the end the life so prescribed will be saved. Hence all these fictitious dogmas are generally promulgated to keep the people in subjection, and to detain them in a fallacious obedience; and a blasphemous covetousness is the damnable root of the whole of them.

Let us look, then, and see what is enjoined and commanded by the Lord, in the law of perfect liberty, and observe it, and abstain from what is forbidden, and from giving attention to laws newly ordained, and this will be enough. Accordingly, what is over and above is not only evil in its origin, but is itself evil, and blinds many. Concerning all vows, promises, and other private observances, let the believer look up to the almighty power of Jesus Christ; let him bend all the strength of his soul to living henceforth in more perfectness, so as to be service-able to the church; let him repent of his past evil life, strengthen within him the purpose of sinning no more; and this, in my opinion, sufficeth to destroy his guilt, and to save him, whatever our superiors may say to the contrary. But in all this, let the believer beware of any insincerity toward God. With regard to the words in Matthew xvi., "Whatsoever ye bind," etc., let the believer demand from the false bishop when he alleges this saying of our Lord's, if his own life of holiness, by its resemblance to the life of Peter, is such as to make him a true vicar of Peter. If the presumptuous hypocrite shall impudently affirm that it is so, ask him to show the similarity of his life to that of Peter, more especially in the grace given him to work miracles, and in the lowliness of his poverty. Peter presumed not on the possession of such power, how then can this hypocrite claim it? And since he cannot prove him-self a true vicar of Christ, or a member of the Church of Christ, what is it to him that Christ promised this power to the blessed Peter, seeing he is neither Peter, nor by the lowness and holiness of his life the vicar of Peter?

23   *John Hus*

Hus, the Bohemian who was influenced by Wyclif, was burned at the stake by the Council of Constance for heresy. This is one of the letters Hus wrote while in prison. This letter is edited and translated by Matthew Spinka, author of John Hus *at the Council of Constance.*

JOHN HUS TO THE MEMBERS OF THE UNIVERSITY OF PRAGUE

[June 27, 1415]

Honorable and in Christ Jesus dearly beloved masters, bachelors, and students of the University of Prague! I exhort you for the sake of the most kind Jesus Himself, that you love one another, root out schisms, and promote the honor of God before all else, keeping me in memory that I always sought the advancement of the university to the honor of God, that I grieved over your discords and excesses, and wished to unite our illustrious nation into one. And see how some of my dearest friends, for whom I would have risked my life, turned exceedingly bitter against me, afflicting me with calumnious vilifications and finally with a bitter death! May the omnipotent God forgive them, for they know not what they have done. I pray for them with a sincere heart that He may spare them.

Moreover, dearly beloved in Christ Jesus, stand in the truth you have learned, for it conquers all and is mighty to eternity. You should also know that I have neither revoked nor abjured a single article. The Council desired that I declare that all and every article drawn from my books is false. I refused unless they should show its falsity by Scripture. I said that I detest whatever false sense exists in any of the articles, and commit it to the correction of the Lord Jesus Christ, Who knows my sincere intention and does not interpret it in a wrong sense which I do not intend. I exhort you also in the Lord that whatever false sense you may be able to discern in any of those articles, that you relinquish them, but always preserve the truth that is intended. Pray God for me, and greet one another in holy peace.

Master John Hus,

SOURCE. Matthew Spinka, *John Hus at the Council of Constance* (New York: Columbia University Press, 1955), pp. 289–290. Reprinted by permission of the publisher.

in chains and in prison, already standing on the
shore of the present life, expecting tomorrow a
terrible death which will, I hope, purge my sins,
by the grace of God find no heresy in me; for I
confess with all my heart whatever truth is
worthy of belief.

Written on Thursday before the vigil of St. Peter.

I Pray you, love Bethlehem and appoint
Havlík in my place; for I hope that the Lord is
with him. Amen.

I commend Peter of Mladoňovice to you, my
most faithful and most constant comforter and
upholder.

PART VI

Authority and Dissent

Christianity is unusual among religions in that it has traditionally placed at least as high a value upon abstract truth as upon morality, ritual, or direct religious experience like mysticism. As a result of this attitude, derived in large part from Greek rationalism, doctrinal orthodoxy has been more important than anything else in defining what—and who—is Christian. It was generally assumed by medieval theologians that one who denied the teaching of the Church (which from the eleventh century was increasingly defined as the Roman Church and identified with the papacy) was automatically cut off from communion with the pope and with his fellow Christians: he was excommunicated. Since the Church was held to be the mystical body of Christ, a heretic was considered cut off from the body of Christ, and therefore from the life of God. As a result, he became a limb of the Devil. He was spiritually an outcast and, in a society dominated by spiritual values, usually a social outcast as well.

But these definitions, and their strict application, are to a great extent products of the increasing institutionalization of the Church, and the concomitant development of canon law, from the latter eleventh century onwards. In the early Middle Ages, heretics were usually treated with leniency. Through the eleventh century very few heretics were punished officially with more than ecclesiastical censure, though some were beaten or killed by angry mobs. The first execution for heresy occurred at Orléans in 1022 by order of the secular authority, King Robert the Pious, and such executions remained rare until towards the end of the twelfth century. At that time the increasing rigidity and efficiency of Church organization, combined with the multiplication of heresies and heretics, caused more drastic measures to be taken. The episcopal inquisition was begun in 1184 and the papal inquisition in the 1220s. Bishops and inquisitors (usually friars, particularly Dominicans) sought out heretics and presented them to the ecclesiastical courts. If they were found guilty, they were delivered over to the secular arm "for appropriate attention": *animadversione debita*. This phrase, a euphemism for a death sentence, allowed the Church to claim that it never executed heretics. The job was done for it by the secular rulers, who introduced legislation for this purpose: Pedro of Aragon decreed death for heretics in 1197, and the emperor Frederick II followed suit in 1224. In the meanwhile, by preaching a crusade against the heretics, Innocent III had already in effect approved the penalty. In the bull *Ad extirpanda* of 1252, Alexander IV allowed the use of torture to secure confessions; and England followed the oppressive legislation of the Continent in the statute *De haeretico comburendo* of 1401. The intolerance of the later medieval Church continued into the sixteenth century, when it was matched by the intolerance of the Protestant Reformers, the result being more than a century of religious warfare.

24   *Lucius III : Ad abolendam*

Lucius III was one of the most vigorous popes in combating heresy. He presided over the Council of Verona in 1184 at which the bishops were enjoined to seek out and prosecute heretics in their dioceses. The same year Lucius issued the decree Ad abolendam. *The following translation is by G. G. Coulton, author of* The Death Penalty for Heresy *from 1184 to 1921.*

All those who, concerning the Sacrament of our Lord Jesus Christ's body and Blood, or baptism, or the confession of sins, or matrimony or the other Sacraments of the Church, fear not to think or teach otherwise than the holy Roman Church preacheth and observeth— and generally whomsoever the said Roman Church, or the separate Bishops in their dioceses with the counsel of their clergy, or the clergy themselves, when the see is vacant, with the counsel (if this be proper) of the neighboring Bishops—we bind with the chain of perpetual anathema. None the less do we decree by this present ordinance, that whosoever be manifestly caught in heresy, if he be a cleric, or darkened over with any shadow of religion, he shall be stripped of the prerogative of the whole ecclesiastical order, and thus, despoiled of all church office and benefice, be left to the judgment of the secular power, to be punished with the penalty that is his due; unless, immediately after he be taken in error, he consent to return of his own accord to the unity of the Catholic faith, and to abjure his error publicly at the decision of the Bishop of his diocese, and to make due satisfaction. Let a layman, on the other hand, (unless, as aforesaid, he abjure his heresy and make satisfaction and flee hastily to the ortho- dox faith) be left to the arbitrament of the secular judge, to receive due vengeance in proportion to the quality of his crime. Those, again, who are found branded by suspicion only, shall be subjected to a like sen- tence unless at the Bishop's decision they have proved their own innocence by due process of purgation, according to the consideration of the suspicion and the quality of the person. We decree that those

SOURCE. Lucius III, *Ad abolendam*, trans. by Coulton in G. G. Coulton, *The Death Penalty for Heresy from 1184–1921* (London: Simpkin, Marshall, Hamilton, Kent & Co., 1924), pp. 49–50.

also who, after abjuration of their error, or after (as aforesaid) they have purged themselves by the examination of their own bishop, have been caught relapsing into the heresy they have abjured, shall be left to secular judgment without any hearing whatsoever.

We decree also that counts, barons, rectors and consuls of cities and other places, according to the admonition of their Bishops, shall promise by the taking of a formal oath that, when required by them [the Bishops], they will *bona-fide*, according to their office and power, help the Church faithfully and efficaciously against the heretics and their accomplices. If they are unwilling to observe this, let them be despoiled of the honour which they hold, and not be promoted on any account to others, while they themselves are none the less to be bound by excommunication, and their lands are to be laid under ecclesiastical interdict. Again, the city which thinks fit to resist these statutes, or which, contrary to the Bishop's warning, neglects to punish resisters, let this city be cut off from intercourse with other cities, and know that it must be deprived of episcopal dignity. Again, if there are any who, exempt from the authority of diocesan jurisdiction, are subject only to the power of the Apostolic see, let them none the less, in these statutes against heretics, be subject to the judgement of the Bishops; and let them, notwithstanding the privileges of their liberty, render obedience unto the Bishops in that district [or matter] as unto delegates from the Apostolic See.

25   *The Fourth Lateran Council*

The Fourth Lateran Council of 1215, under the presidency of Pope Innocent III, issued the following general condemnation of heretics (especially Catharists and Valdesians) and their abettors. The council also reminds the bishops of their duties in hunting down the heretics. The following is taken from Colman J. Barry, Readings in Church History.

We excommunicate and anathematize every heresy that raises itself against the holy, orthodox and Catholic faith which we have above ex-

SOURCE. Henry J. Schroeder, O.P., trans. *Disciplinary Decrees of the General Councils* (St. Louis: Herder, 1937). Reprinted in Colman J. Barry, *Readings in Church History* (Westminster, Md.: Newman Press, 1960), vol. I, pp. 440–442. Reprinted by permission of the Newman Press.

plained; condemning all heretics under whatever names they may be known, for while they have different faces, they are nevertheless bound to each other by their tails, since in all of them vanity is a common element. Those condemned, being handed over to the secular rulers or their bailiffs, let them be abandoned, to be punished with due justice, clerics being first degraded from their orders. As to the property of the condemned, if they are laymen, let it be confiscated; if clerics, let it be applied to the churches from which they received revenues. But those who are only suspected, due consideration being given to the nature of the suspicion and the character of the person, unless they prove their innocence by a proper defense, let them be anathematized and avoided by all until they have made suitable satisfaction; but if they have been under excommunication for one year, then let them be condemned as heretics. Secular authorities, whatever office they may hold, shall be admonished and induced and if necessary compelled by ecclesiastical censure, that as they wish to be esteemed and numbered among the faithful, so for the defense of the faith they ought publicly to take an oath that they will strive in good faith and to the best of their ability to exterminate in the territories subject to their jurisdiction all heretics pointed out by the Church; so that whenever anyone shall have assumed authority, whether spiritual or temporal, let him be bound to confirm this decree by oath. But if a temporal ruler, after having been requested and admonished by the Church, should neglect to cleanse his territory of this heretical foulness, let him be excommunicated by the metropolitan and the other bishops of the province. If he refuses to make satisfaction within a year, let the matter be made known to the supreme pontiff, that he may declare the ruler's vassals absolved from their allegiance and may offer the territory to be ruled by Catholics, who on the extermination of the heretics may possess it without hindrance and preserve it in the purity of faith; the right, however, of the chief ruler is to be respected so long as he offers no obstacle in this matter and permits freedom of action. The same law is to be observed in regard to those who have no chief rulers (that is, are independent). Catholics who have girded themselves with the cross for the extermination of the heretics, shall enjoy the indulgences and privileges granted to those who go in defense of the Holy Land.

We decree that those who give credence to the teachings of the heretics, as well as those who receive, defend, and patronize them, are excommunicated; and we firmly declare that after any one of them has been branded with excommunication, if he has deliberately failed to make satisfaction within a year, let him incur *ipso jure* the stigma of infamy and let him not be admitted to public offices or deliberations, and let him not take part in the election of others to such offices or use his right to give testimony in a court of law. Let him also be intestable, that he may not have the free exercise of making a will, and let him be deprived of the right of inheritance. Let no one be urged to give an account to him in any matter, but let him be urged to give an account to others. If perchance he be a judge, let his decisions have no force, nor let any cause be brought to his attention. If he be an advocate, let his assistance by no means be sought. If a notary, let the instruments drawn up by him be considered worthless, for, the author being condemned, let them enjoy a similar fate. In all similar cases we command that the same be observed. If, however, he be a cleric, let him be deposed from every office and benefice, that the greater the fault the graver may be the punishment inflicted.

If any refuse to avoid such after they have been ostracized by the Church, let them be excommunicated till they have made suitable satisfaction. Clerics shall not give the sacraments of the Church to such pestilential people, nor shall they presume to give them Christian burial, or to receive their alms or offerings; otherwise they shall be deprived of their office, to which they may not be restored without a special indult of the Apostolic See. Similarly, all regulars, on whom also this punishment may be imposed, let their privileges be nullified in that diocese in which they have presumed to perpetrate such excesses.

But since some, under the "appearance of godliness, but denying the power thereof," as the Apostle says, arrogate to themselves the authority to preach, as the same Apostle says: "How shall they preach unless they be sent?", all those prohibited or not sent, who, without the authority of the Apostolic See or of the Catholic bishop of the locality, shall presume to usurp the office of preaching either publicly or privately, shall be excommunicated and unless they amend, and the sooner the better, they shall be visited with a further suitable penalty. We add, moreover, that every archbishop or bishop should himself or through his archdeacon or some other suitable persons, twice or at least once a year make the rounds of his diocese in which report has it that heretics dwell, and there compel three or more men of good character or, if it should be deemed advisable, the entire neighborhood, to swear that if anyone know of the presence there of heretics or others holding secret assemblies, or differing from the common way of the faithful in faith and morals, they will make them known to the bishop. The latter shall then call together before him those accused, who, if they do not purge themselves of the matter of which they are accused, or if after the rejection of their error they lapse into their former wickedness, shall be canonically punished. But if any of them by damnable obstinacy should disapprove of the oath and should perchance be unwilling to swear, from this very fact let them be regarded as heretics.

We wish, therefore, and in virtue of obedience strictly command, that to carry out these instructions effectively the bishops exercise throughout their dioceses a scrupulous vigilance if they wish to escape canonical punishment. If from sufficient evidence it is apparent that a bishop is negligent or remiss in cleansing his diocese of the ferment of heretical wickedness, let him be deposed from the episcopal office and let another, who will and can confound heretical depravity, be substituted.

26   *Innocent III and the Heretics*

The following is taken from Herbert Grundmann, Ketzergeschichte des Mittelalters.

[Pope Innocent III was one of the first popes to take thoroughgoing measures against heresy.] He was convinced that it was necessary to determine much more carefully than has been done in the past who was orthodox and who was invincibly heretical, in order not to condemn the innocent along with the guilty, the grain along with the tares, which would hurt the Church more than hurting heresy. As soon as he became pope, he urged the bishops wherever possible to reconcile to the Church those members of orders of religious poverty who were sincere and who had good will toward the Church, in order the better to fight against those unbelievers who were stubborn in their resistance. He expressed this in terms of an analogy: a doctor, in order to heal that part of the body which is capable of being saved, is obliged to cut out that which is malignant, in order that the malig-

SOURCE. Herbert Grundmann, *Ketzergeschichte des Mittelatters* (Göttingen: Vanden-hoeck & Ruprecht, 1963), pp. G34–G39. Translated for this volume by Jeffrey B. Russell. Reprinted by permission of the publisher.

nancy may not grow. Often in his expostulations he used the words of St. Luke (X, 34), saying that a wound would be treated first with oil and then with wine, that is, first with mildness and then with drastic measures. Or he would use the words of St. Matthew (xviii, 12–13), comparing the problem of heresy with bringing back the wandering sheep into the herd, or with the reception of the Prodigal Son (Luke, xv, 11ff). He acted according to these principles in coming to an agreement with the Humiliati, who had previously been condemned as heretics, and also with certain of the Valdesians. At the beginning of 1207 the Spanish Bishop Diego of Osma, while on his way home from Rome with his companion Dominic, had debated publicly with some Valdesians. The leader of the Valdesians, Durand of Osca, also a Spaniard, was prepared to re-enter the Church with his followers, though not to give up their life of wandering, preaching, and poverty. These former heretics went to Rome, underwent a doctrinal examination, and swore to a profession of faith very similar to that to which Valdes had subscribed thirty years before. They promised to obey the pope and the bishops, to recognize the power of priests to administer the sacraments whether or not they were morally worthy, and they agreed not to consider swearing and the shedding of blood as necessarily mortal sins, even though they themselves continued to be exempt from taking oaths and from military service against other Christians. Under these conditions—not dissimilar to the original teaching of the Valdesians—those who reconverted to Christianity were recognized by the pope as a new and acceptable society of poor and wandering preachers: the *Pauperes Catholici*, so called to distinguish them from the heretical "Poor Men of Lyon." A cardinal was declared their protector, just as was done later with the Fransciscans. . . .

Innocent III's policy of bringing heretics back into the Church by encouraging them to join the evangelical and apostolic movements of poverty within the Church largely succeeded, thanks to the help of the Fransciscans. The religious impulses that previously had either led into heresy or else had been repressed could now swell a healthy and vigorous spirit within the Church and eventually lead even to the repression of heresy. . . .

[Now follows a discussion of the beginning of the Albigensian Crusade, which of course was a departure from the lenient policies of Innocent III. The ultimate rationale for the Albigensian Crusade was that if it was impossible to persuade people through peaceful means to rejoin the Church, then the only other means at the

Church's disposal was force.] At the beginning of 1208 Peter of Castelnau, a papal legate in the south of France, was murdered after a meeting with Count Raymond VI of Toulouse, who was a supporter of the heretics. With the death of Castelnau, the pope, who had unsuccessfully tried to encourage the king of France to intervene, saw no other alternative than to call a crusade against the heretics of southern France exactly as he would have called a crusade against the infidels. This Albigensian Crusade, which for twenty years ravaged the previously fertile countryside, soon escaped papal control and became a simple power struggle over the territories of the County of Toulouse and neighboring districts, until they finally were annexed by force to the domains of the king of France.

27 The Synod of Toulouse

The following are the regulations of the Synod of Toulouse concerning the Inquisition, from Conciliengeschichte.

1. Bishops must bind under oath when necessary in each parish, within and outside a city, a priest and two or more lay people of good reputation to diligently, faithfully, and often search out heretics in their parishes, individual suspicious houses, subterranean rooms and additions to houses, and other hiding places. If they discover a heretic, follower, patron, or protector of heretics, they must, taking precaution that they do not escape, quickly notify the bishop and mayor of the place or his bailiff so they will be duly punished (command of the episcopal inquisition according to the practice of the synods of Verona, Bourges, Narbonne, and the twelfth general synod).

2. Exempt abbots, who are not subject to episcopal jurisdiction, must act in the same way as the bishops.

3. The governors of the respective districts should order diligent search of country residences, houses, and forests for heretics and destroy their hiding places.

SOURCE. Conrad Zimmerman, trans., *Conciliengeschichte* (Freiburg im Breisgau: Herder, 1886). Reprinted in Colman J. Barry, *Readings in Church History* (Westminster, Md.: Newman Press, 1960), vol. V, pp. 980–986.

4. Whoever, allowing a heretic to stay on his property either for money or any other cause, if he confesses or is convicted, loses his property forever and his body is handed over to the civil authority for punishment.

5. He also is subject to legal punishment whose property, although without his knowledge but by negligence, has become an abode of heretics.

6. The house where a heretic is found must be torn down and the property must be confiscated.

7. The bailiff who lives in a suspicious place and is not diligent in searching for heretics loses his office and is not permitted to be employed either there or in any other place.

8. In order to prevent an innocent person from being punished or slanderously accused of heresy we command that no one shall be punished as a heretic or follower of heresy before he is so declared by a bishop or other clerical persons.

9. All are permitted to search for heretics in others' territories, and the bailiffs must help them. The king can, accordingly, search for heretics in the territory of the count of Toulouse, and the count of Toulouse in the king's land.

10. If one who is tainted with heresy voluntarily gives up the heresy he is not allowed to remain in the house where he formerly lived in case the house was under suspicion of heresy. He must be moved into a Catholic house which is free from suspicion. Besides, he must wear two crosses on his coat; the one on the right and the other on the left, and of a different color from his coat. Such persons cannot hold public office or be admitted to legal actions unless they are fully re-instated after due penance by the pope or his legate.

11. Whoever has involuntarily returned to the Church, through fear of death or for any other reason, must be imprisoned by the bishop so he can perform his penance or not be able to seduce others. Whoever retains his property must, by order of the prelate, provide for his own necessities. If he possesses nothing, then the prelate must provide for him.

12. All members of a parish shall vow to the bishop under oath that they will preserve the Catholic faith and will persecute heretics according to their power. This oath must be renewed every two years.

13. Males and females who have attained the use of reason must confess their sins to a priest three times a year, or with their priest's

permission to another priest. They must perform the imposed penances humbly and according to their strength and receive the holy sacrament of the Eucharist three times a year. Whoever does not do this is under suspicion of being a heretic.

14. Lay people are not permitted to possess the books of the Old and New Testament, only the Psalter, Breviary, or the Little Office of the Blessed Virgin, and these books not in the vernacular language.

15. Whoever is accused of heresy or is only suspected of heresy is not permitted to practice his profession as a doctor. When a sick person has received Holy Communion from his priest he must be careful that no heretic or one suspected of heresy visit him, for terrible things have already happened through such visits. . . .

17. No prelate, baron or other superiors shall entrust the office of bailiff or steward to any heretic or follower of heresy, nor keep in his service one who has been condemned or suspected of heresy.

18. He is accused of heresy or is suspected of heresy who has been legally proved by good and honorable people before a bishop of having a bad reputation. . . .

42. Women who own castles or fortresses are not permitted to marry enemies of the faith and the peace. . . .

44. Whoever is too poor to employ a lawyer has to be provided with one if necessary by the curia.

45. Pastors must explain these regulations to their parishioners four times a year.

28   *Secular Laws Against Heresy*

a. The Legislation of Frederick II. *The following account is by Henry Charles Lea,* History of the Inquisition of the Middle Ages.

In a series of edicts dating from 1220 to 1239 Frederick enacted a complete and pitiless code of persecution, based upon the Lat-

SOURCE. Henry Charles Lea, *A History of the Inquisition of the Middle Ages* (Harpers, 1888) (New York: Russell & Russell, 1955), pp. 321–323. Reprinted by permission of the publisher.

eran canons. Those who were merely suspected of heresy were required to purge themselves at command of the Church, under penalty of being deprived of civil rights and placed under the imperial ban; while, if they remained in this condition for a year, they were to be condemed as heretics. Heretics of all sects were outlawed; and when condemned as such by the Church they were to be delivered to the secular arm to be burned. If, through fear of death, they recanted, they were to be thrust in prison for life, there to perform penance. If they relapsed into error, thus showing that their conversion had been fictitious, they were to be put to death. All the property of the heretic was confiscated and his heirs disinherited. His children, to the second generation, were declared ineligible to any positions of emolument or dignity, unless they should win mercy by betraying their father or some other heretic. All "credentes," fautors, defenders, receivers, or advocates of heretics were banished forever, their property confiscated, and their descendants subjected to the same disabilities as those of heretics. Those who defended the errors of heretics were to be treated as heretics unless, on admonition, they mended their ways. The houses of heretics and their receivers were to be destroyed, never to be rebuilt. Although the evidence of a heretic was not receivable in court, yet an exception was made in favor of the faith, and it was to be held good against another heretic. All rulers and magistrates, present or future, were required to swear to exterminate with their utmost ability all whom the Church might designate as heretics, under pain of forfeiture of office. The lands of any temporal lord who neglected, for a year after summons by the Church, to clear them of heresy, were exposed to the occupancy of any Catholics who, after extirpating the heretics, were to possess them in peace without prejudice to the rights of the suzerain, provided he had offered no opposition. When the papal Inquisition was commenced, Frederic hastened, in 1232, to place the whole machinery of the State at the command of the inquisitors, who were authorized to call upon any official to capture whomsoever they might designate as a heretic, and hold him in prison until the church should condemn him, when he was to be put to death.

This fiendish legislation was hailed by the Church with acclamation, and was not allowed to remain, like its predecessors, a dead letter. The coronation-edict of 1220 was sent by Honorius to the University of Bologna to be read and taught as a part of practical law. It was consequently embodied in the authoritative compilation of the feudal customs, and its most stringent enactments were incorporated in the Civil Code. The whole series of edicts was subsequently promulgated by successive popes in repeated bulls, commanding all states and cities to inscribe these laws irrevocably in their local statute-books. It became the duty of the inquisitors to see that this was done, to swear all magistrates and officials to enforce them, and to compel their obedience by the free use of excommunication. In 1222, when the magistrates of Rieti adopted laws conflicting with them, Honorius at once ordered the offenders removed from office; in 1227 the people of Rimini resisted, but were coerced to submission; in 1253, when some of the Lombard cities demurred, Innocent IV promptly ordered the inquisitors to subdue them; in 1254 Asti peacefully accepted them as part of its local laws; Como followed the example, September 10, 1255; and in the recension of the laws of Florence made as late as 1355, they still appear as an integral part. Finally, they were incorporated in the latest additions to the Corpus Juris as part of the canon law itself, and, technically speaking, they may be regarded as in force to the present day.

This virtually provided for a very large portion of Europe, extending from Sicily to the North Sea. The western regions made haste to follow the pious example. Coincident with the Treaty of Paris, in 1229, was an *ordonnance* issued in the name of the boy-king, Louis IX., giving efficient assistance by the royal officials to the Church in its efforts to purge the land of heresy. In the territories which remained to Count Raymond his vacillating course gave rise to much dissatisfaction, until, in 1234, he was compelled to enact, with the consent of his prelates and barons, a statute drawn up by the fanatic Raymond du Fauga of Toulouse, which embodied all the practical points of Frederic's legislation, and decreed confiscation against every one who failed, when called upon, to aid the Church in the capture and detention of heretics. In the compilations and law books of the latter half of the century we see the system thoroughly established as the law of the whole land, and in 1315 Louis le Hutin formally adopted the edicts of Frederic and made them valid throughout France.

b. The Sachsenspiegel *(1215–1235), a German law code, includes the following (translation by Edward P. Cheyney).*

OLD LOW GERMAN LAWS AGAINST HERESY, DER SACHSENSPIEGEL, 1215–1235

Where persons are believed to be heretics, they shall be accused before the spiritual court, for they should in the first place be tried by ecclesiastics. When they are convicted they shall be taken in hand by the secular court, which shall sentence them as is right; that is to say, they shall be burned at the stake. If, however, the judge protects them, or makes any illegal concessions and does not sentence them, he shall be excommunicated, and that in the most severe form. This shall be done by a bishop. The delinquent judge shall, moreover, be judged by his superior temporal judge, if he have one, as he himself should have judged the heretic. In case a feudal prince does not bring heretics to judgment, but protects them, the ecclesiastical court shall excommunicate him. If such prince does not yield within the space of a year, his bishop, who excommunicated him, shall report his evil deeds to the pope and the length of time he has remained excommunicated for the same. Then shall he [the pope] with propriety deprive him of his princely office and of all his dignities. The pope shall bring his sentence to the notice of his king and his other judges. These shall substantiate the sentence of the pope with their sentence. The offender shall be deprived of all his goods, his fiefs and all his worldly honors. Thus shall lords and poor men be judged. The fitness of this is thus shown.

There was once a pope at Rome called Zacharias. In his time there was a king of France called Lescandus who protected the heretics unlawfully. He was king before King Pippin, King Charles' father. Him the pope deposed from his kingship and from all this honors, and Pippin became king in the stead during his natural life. We read, too, that Pope Innocent deposed King Otto of the Roman Empire on account of his ill deeds. This the popes have a right to do, as God spake to Jeremiah, saying. "I have set thee over all the nations and over all the kingdoms to judge."

SOURCE. Trans. by Edward P. Cheyney, in *Original Sources of European History* (Philadelphia: University of Pennsylvania Press, 1902). Reprinted in Colman J. Barry, *Readings in Church History* (Westminster, Md.: Newman Press, 1960), vol. III, pp. 542–543.

PART VII

Personality, Society, and Dissent

Though religious dissent was essentially religious in inspiration, it can be thoroughly understood only when its psychological and sociological context had been elucidated. The preaching of heresy required a certain amount of psychological tension—or courage—for individual honesty and dissent has never been popular, particularly in a conservative society like that of the Middle Ages. The historian, though refraining from facile Freudianism and from reading into the sources more than they can bear, will increasingly utilize the insights of modern psychology in understanding heretical leaders, and social psychology will help him to understand the movements that followed these heresiarchs. Sociology will help him to understand the form and functions of these movements in society. To what extent were heretical movements correlated with open social unrest? To what extent did they express hidden social tensions in theological or spiritual language? What kinds of people tended to attach themselves to heretical movements? In what kinds of economic environment were heretical movements likely to arise? Why were medieval heretical movements relatively isolated and limited in scope, as compared to the widespread dissent during the Protestant Reformation? These are some of the sociological questions that will be asked.

29   *Dissent and Millennarianism*

*Norman Cohn saw in the Christian millennarianism of the Middle Ages the fore-
runner of modern Marxism.*

Between the close of the eleventh century and the first half
of the sixteenth it repeatedly happened in Europe that the desire
of the poor to imporve the material conditions of their lives
became transfused with phantasies of a new Paradise on earth, a
world purged of suffering and sin, a Kingdom of the Saints.
The history of those centuries was of course sprinkled with innumerable struggles between the privileged and the less privileged,
risings of towns against their overlords, of artisans against merchant
capitalists, of peasants against nobles. Usually those risings had
strictly limited aims—the securing of specific rights, the removal of
specific grievances—or else (like the famous *Jacquerie*) were mere
outbreaks of destructive rage provoked by sheer misery. But risings
could also occur which had quite a different scope. The Middle Ages
had inherited from Antiquity—from the Jews and the early Christians—a tradition of prophecy which during those same centuries took
on a fresh and exuberant vitality. In the language of theology—
which seems here the most appropriate language—there existed an
eschatology, or body of doctrine concerning the final state of the world,
which was chiliastic in the most general sense of the term—meaning
that it foretold a Millennium, not necessarily limited to a thousand
years and indeed not necessarily limited at all, in which the world
would be inhabited by a humanity at once perfectly good and perfectly
happy. Offering so much solace of a kind which the official teaching
of the medieval Church withheld, this eschatology came to exercise a
powerful and enduring fascination. Generation after generation was
seized at least intermittently by a tense expectation of some sudden,
miraculous event in which the world would be utterly transformed,
some prodigious final struggle between the hosts of Christ and the

SOURCE. Norman Cohn, *The Pursuit of the Millennium* (London: Martin Secker
& Warburg Limited; New York: Harper & Row, Inc., 1957), pp. xiii-xv. Reprinted
by permission of the publishers.

hosts of Antichrist through which history would attain its fulfilment and justification. Although it would be a gross over-simplification to identify the world of chiliastic exaltation with the world of social unrest, there were many times when needy and discontented masses were captured by some millennial prophet. And when that happened movements were apt to arise which, though relatively small and short-lived, can be seen in retrospect to bear a startling resemblance to the great totalitarian movements of our day.

Such a comparison is bound to arouse misgivings. Is it more than a mere retrojecting on to a vanished civilisation of preoccupations which in reality belong to today alone? If I think so, that is not because I would deny that in the unpredictable kaleidoscope which we call history each transient constellation has its unique and irreductible particularity. But in the history of social behavior there certainly are some patterns which in their main outlines recur again and again, revealing as they do so similarities which become ever more recognisable. And this is no where more evident than in the case of highly emotional mass movements such as from the subject-matter of this book. It has happened countless times that people have grouped themselves in millennial movements of one kind or another. It has happened at many different periods of history, in many different parts of the world and in societies which have differed greatly in their technologies and institutions, values and beliefs. These movements have varied in tone from the most violent aggressiveness to the mildest pacifism and in aim from the most ethereal spirituality to the most earthbound materialism; there is no counting the possible ways of imagining the Millennium and the route to it. But similarities can present themselves as well as differences; and the more carefully one compares the outbreaks of militant social chiliasm during the later Middle Ages with modern totalitarian movements the more remarkable the similarities appear. The old symbols and the old slogans have indeed disappeared, to be replaced by new ones; but the structure of the basic phantasies seems to have changed scarcely at all.

The time seems ripe for an examination of those remote foreshadowings of present commotions. If such an enquiry can throw no appreciable light on the workings of established totalitarian states, it might, and I think does, throw considerable light on the sociology and psychology of totalitarian movements in their revolutionary heyday. Nor, from this point of view, is there any call to distinguish overmuch between what so far have been the two major forms of totalitarianism, Communism on the one hand and

German National Socialism on the other. Admittedly it seems a far cry from the atavism, the crude tribalism, the vulgar irrationalism and open sadism of the Nazis to the ostensible humanitarian and universalist, scientific and rational outlook of the Communists—and still it is true that both these movements share certain features so extraordinary as to suggest the emergence of a form of politics vastly different from any known in the past. It is precisely these features which are best elucidated by reference to that subterranean revolutionary eschatology which so often sent tremors through the massive structure of medieval society.

The genesis of that eschatology has not so far been made the subject of a detailed study. The more strictly religious sects which appeared and disappeared during those same centuries have received ample attention. Countless books have been written about the Cathars, whose Gnostic religion once flourished over large areas of of southern Europe, and about the Waldensians, whom some regard as remote harbingers of the Reformation. Much has also been written about those most unworldly of chiliasts, the Franciscan Spirituals. But relatively little attention has been given to the story of how, again and again over some four and a half centuries, apocalyptic lore became charged with social aspirations, animosities and anxieties to which in turn it gave a new and peculiar dynamism. Though there is no lack of excellent monographs dealing with single episodes or aspects, the story as a whole has remained untold.

30   *Marxist Interpretations*

Ernst Werner of the Karl-Marx University of Leipzig has emerged as the leading orthodox Marxist historian of medieval dissent. He and his colleague Martin Erbstösser collaborated in the volume Ideologische Probleme des mittelalterlichen Plebjertums. *Erbstösser wrote the following selection from Chapter One.*

In the second half of the thirteenth century another heresy was

SOURCE. Ernst Werner and Martin Erbstösser, *Ideologische Probleme des mittelalterlichen Plebjertums* (Berlin: Akademie-Verlag, 1960). Translated for the volume by Jeffrey B. Russell. Reprinted by permission of the publisher.

added to those already troubling feudal society: the pantheistic sect of the Brethren and Sisters of the Free Spirit. Originating at the beginning of the thirteenth century, this sect had become fully developed by 1300, with its centers on both sides of the Rhine and in the Netherlands. Bourgeois historians have been relatively neglectful of this sect and have yet to produce a general interpretation of it. Rather, they have concerned themselves with only two parts of the whole question: the origin and development of the ideology of the heretics and their relationship to the Beghards and Beguines. The superficial nature of the bourgeois interpretation of even these two questions arises from the theoretical problems inherent in the subject. The origins of the pantheistic ideology of the Free Spirit is closely bound to a series of other ideological phenomena, of which the most important were the decomposition of Catharist ideology in western Europe and the growth of mystical speculation among the Beguines of the Rhineland and the Netherlands. A long and still unresolved debate among intellectual historians has centered upon the origin and the influence of these movements on the Free Spirit. Similar theoretical problems accompanied the investigation of the external relationship between the Brethren of the Free Spirit and the Beguines. Because of fluctuations in membership and beliefs, the sect of the Free Spirit is difficult to define. Yet the sources again and again point to its close relationships with the Beguines. Historians have also pointed out the relationship between the Free Spirit and other movements of apostolic poverty that, like that of the Beguines and Beghards, were on the periphery of orthodoxy. Emphasis upon this important point therefore seems completely justified. However, the traditional approach, in spite of the many important studies it has produced on particular aspects of the program, has not achieved a real grasp of the essence of this heretical movement. The chief cause of this failure is the idealistic assumptions of the bourgeois historians. They have, in their treatment of the first part of the problem, dwelt upon intellectual connections and relationships, and, in their treatment of the second, emphasized superficial phenomena, organizational forms, and other similar questions. With only a few exceptions, they have either ignored the social concerns of the sect or at least treated them only peripherally. Haupt's assertion that it is impossible, because of the fluctuating character of and variety of influences on the sect, to write a general history of it, is typical of the old school.

At the tenth International Historical Congress at Rome in 1955, Herbert Grundmann described the future direction of bourgeois research on the Free Spirit: "[The phenomenon of antinomian pan-theism] cannot be understood in terms of external influences, of social causes, of moral decay, or of lay misunderstanding or abuse of philo-sophical or theological speculations. All these may have had some part in the phenomenon, but they are only symptoms of a crisis in Christian life and thought, a crisis in which ancient traditions were no longer merely believed but pursued, with all their potentialities, to extremes, allegedly in order to find new ways to a higher religious fulfillment, indeed to achieve the union of men with God." Here Grundmann, as is not at all surprising when one considers his earlier work, goes farther down the road of the history of ideas and with marked bias rejects con-sideration of all other historical viewpoints. Extraordinary narrow-ness on the part of a bourgeois historian who so readily reproaches Marxist historians with narrowmindedness. In any event Grund-mann's approach to research is not clearly distinguished from other bourgeois scholarly opinions. Even those bourgeois historians who recognize a social element in their treatment of the problem of sects fail in the last analysis to explain heretical ideology in terms of the social situation of the sectaries, instead treating the social aspect as an isolat-ed phenomenon. Such interpretations fail to grasp that the heretical ideology springs from the particular "social factors" there present.

The present work is designed to present an interpretation that differs from bourgeois, idealist historiography on the fundamental question of the relationship between social position and social con-sciousness. For in the last analysis, ideas and consciousness are, not-withstanding their contributions to action, only a reflection of social reality in the brains of men. Drawing upon deep historical experience, Karl Marx has pronounced that: "One must distinguish between the material, scientifically provable conflict among economic conditions of production on the one hand, and on the other the legal, political, religious, artistic, or philosophical—in short ideological—forms whereby men seek to understand and express this conflict."

That means, in terms of our problem, that the ideologies of "reli-gious" or heretical movements are forms of consciousness with which certain groups of men react to social or economic changes, or in which they express, in ideological terms, the class conflicts and struggles that arise from these changes. During the Middle Ages, ideological expres-sions of class struggles took predominantly religious forms, for the churches of western Europe dominated the whole ideological super-structure with their dogmas and institutional organization, thereby providing ideological support for the feudal order. Friedrich Engels' analysis of the situation before the Peasants' War in Germany is apposite: "It is clear that in this part of a society all general attacks upon feudalism were necessarily at the same time attacks upon the Church and that all revolutionary social and political doctrines were necessarily at the same time theological heresies. In order for the existing social conditions to be effectively challenged, their religious manifestations had to be attacked as well."

The areas of attack vary with economic and social conditions, but in their essence medieval religious movements are similar, for they pit certain classes or groups of people against existing social conditions, yet never go as far as abnegating religion altogether: they limited themselves, rather, to a criticism of dogmas, ecclesiastical institutions, or ecclesiastical organization—a criticism within the framework of Christianity that is defined as heresy. Or, again, they may merely emphasize a particular element of Catholic belief that serves their particular purposes but that is uncongenial to currently prevailing religious views or customs.

These are the sorts of theoretical questions that this study will emphasize. We shall by no means ignore the question (left open by bourgeois historians) of the origin of the heretical ideology. When men accept ideas (in this case heretical ones), they are adopting a previously existing body of thought and adding to and developing it until it has taken the shape that is proper to the socio-economic conditions of the time. Friedrich Engels himself wrote a letter to Franz Mehring on the importance of intellectual precedents. But this is by no means a justification of the bourgeois ideological interpretation: in the first place, this kind of intellectual consideration plays only a secondary role in the understanding of the essence of a religious movement like the Free Spirit. In the Second place, a Marxist historian will never view the function and interplay of the elements of an historical situation from the point of view of intellectual history, but rather from the point of view of their function as part of a superstructure built upon social and economic realities. Ernst Werner, for example, has proceeded in this way, and his important evaluations of the ideology of the Free Spirit may be accepted. . . .

The goal of this work is to understand the Heresy of the Free Spirit in its class connections, to present its ideology as an expression of certain societal relationships, and to investigate the influence of the sect and its teachings on the class struggles of the thirteenth and fourteenth centuries. At the same time we shall touch upon several questions concerning the origins of the heretical ideology and upon the emergence of the heresy in the unsympathetic context of feudal society. Particular attention will be paid to defining as closely as possible to what degree the heretical ideology played a fundamentally progressive role in the development of history. We shall also offer a short contribution to the investigation of the essence of sectarianism and to the description of the class conflicts within the feudal order of society in the thirteenth and fourteenth centuries.

31 *Idealist Interpretations*

Most historians of heresy reject the extreme materialism represented by Werner and Erbstösser. While recognizing the importance of economic factors, they hold that the history of heresy is best understood in the framework of intellectual history. The following is from Ilarino da Milano, "Le Eresie Medioevali," Grande Antologia Filosofica.

Heresies are essentially religious phenomena. The various heretical movements and groups that ranged through Europe in the second half of the Middle Ages (from the eleventh through the fifteenth centuries) must be considered as individual manifestations of the religious feeling of those centuries. As indications of general religious feeling, they may be called popular or pragmatic heresies, because they took the forms of movements, groups, and organizations putting into practice a collective variety of spiritual and ascetic activity, although they expressed religious experience in ways beyond the limits of what was then permitted in the Catholic Church and in opposition to its authority and to its dogmatic and moral teachings. . . .

Each heretical manifestation was an attempt at resolving fundamental religious questions, but each also concerned the individual conscience, society in general and even political life in all of its manifestations. This living connection lends a particular social interest to the study and understanding of medieval heresies.

The variety of the heresies is the result of varying conditions: individual initiative, the grievances and attitudes they represented, the

SOURCE. Ilarino da Milano, "Le eresie medioevali," in *Grande Antologia Filosofica* (Milan: Casa Editrice Marzorati, 1954), vol. IV, pp. 1599–1689. Translated for this volume by Jeffrey B. Russell. Reprinted by permission of the publisher.

spiritual and humanitarian motives that inspired them, the nature of their following, and their particular role in particular ecclesiastical, political, and social situations.

It is in the very nature of heretical individualism and of its always more moral than rational inspiration that it was difficult to establish a doctrinal and hierarchical system and to maintain an ordered development and internal growth.

Thus an overall view of medieval heresies is possible only if the diversity of their spiritual elements and social contexts is understood, for these are not open to easy generalization. Nonetheless, the heresies of the Middle Ages in general can be reduced to two major types: Catharism and Valdesianism, that is to say, dualism and evangelical poverty. . . .

All religious movements designated as schismatic or heretical were largely lay in nature and to some extent connected with popular upheaval. However, it is not true, for example, that heretical movements can be explained as the result of attacks against the clergy and feudal nobility by the lower classes, the proletariat, peasants, artisans, petty bourgeois, or simple and illiterate people. In reality heretical movements usually had their greatest influence among those who were identified with very different kinds of groups, for example university teachers and students, or the petty or even the greater nobility. The motivation of these heresies was in fact different for each period and each person. However, they all expressed to some extent a lay solution to the religious problem, since most of these movements were aimed against the priestly monopoly of the sacraments and against the legal authority of the Roman Church. The democratic temper of these movements appears most clearly in this questioning of religious power based upon legalism and hierarchical orders and in the urge to replace such values with values based upon moral virtue, asceticism and divine inspiration, as interpreted by the adherents of the belief. At any rate there was usually a certain pragmatism balancing such democratic ideals, since many of the sects ended by organizing themselves into a hierarchy with authority and powers based upon sacraments and rituals and with a division into two groups, one dominating the sect and the other obliged to obey. . . .

The heretical movements by and large treated society as if it were fundamentally religious and presented their own programs to society as the true religion, or rather as the true interpretation of Christianity. From the very beginning they were antagonistic to, and subversive of, the Catholic Church. In their polemic bitterness they attacked the

Catholic Church for having deviated from true Christian doctrine or for having become too materialistic in its hierarchical institutions, sacraments and rituals, or for having degenerated from the primitive evangelical moral virtues. Against the Catholic Church the heretics often raised the idea of a spiritual, charismatic, eschatological community of believers. The necessity of struggling against the Church and the need to obtain popular support did not permit the heretics to distinguish between a Church instituted by Christ as a legitimate custodian and dispenser of the whole complex nature of Christian revelation on the one hand, and the Church represented in the course of historic events by men who in their priestly and ecclesiastical functions were subject to all of the deficiencies and evils inherent in the world and in any human organization. . . .

In any event the Reformist, spiritual, and charismatic element of heresy brought the heretics into connection with the great movements of moral reform and intellectual progress—the ascetic, monastic, pastoral and sacerdotal movements that the Church has never lacked and that it continued to manifest although the heretics claimed themselves to rivive and even to monopolize them. The efflorescence of popular religiosity in the Middle Ages cannot be limited to heretical movements, because this interpretation would ignore the mainstream of spirituality, mysticism and asceticism, of popular devotion, of moral advance, of reform movements among the hierarchy as well as among the people that appeared in every century including those in which heresy was strong. . . .

The appearance and development of heresies within the framework of medieval religious history are most accurately evaluated historically when taken in context with those spiritual and ascetic movements—monastic, ecclesiastical, and popular—that without revolutionary bitterness and without breaking from the Church developed within the framework of Catholic doctrine and of Christian virtues. In the history of the Church, which through the centuries has often had to employ movements of reform to throw off the burden of decay, the heresies appear as a permanent antithesis to orthodoxy, nourished by forces and motives that vary with the course of events. Or they may appear as an extreme manifestation of a life-giving reaction against corruption. Or they may appear as a temporary infection of otherwise healthy doctrinal and ascetic elements. There is a continuing interest of historians in the history of medieval religious values and their role in offering religious solutions to personal, social, and political problems. Or they may illustrate one phase of the long history of the relationship between the individual and the state in regard to religion and ecclesiastical authority.

32   *Heresy at Florence*

A moderate, scrupulous, and detailed investigation into the economic backgrounds of heresy is highly desirable. Such was presented by Marvin Becker in his article, "Florentine Politics and the Diffusion of Heresy in the Trecento," from which the following is excerpted.

In an age when each socio-economic class sought to justify its existence at the bar of religion, *il popolo minuto* appear to have inaugurated its search for an identity by rejecting religious rationalizations of the upper classes. It might be fair to paraphrase Calmette and suggest that religion was a type of Kantian category in terms of which the men of the Trecento perceived the social world. This fact operated with greater intensity among the membership of *i minuti*. The urban patriciate could look towards a modification of Saint Thomas' Aristotelian political philosophy that would buttress their own republican sentiments. *Il popolo minuto*, on the other hand, had no secularized ideology with which to sanctify their socio-economic aspirations and, therefore, sought for confirmation at the fount of Christianity. This would not only provide them with an element of cohesion but it would also furnish a weapon with which to humble their social superiors.

The teachings of the Spiritual Franciscans, which cast doubt upon the sanctity of private property and contended that wealth was a consequence of original sin, acted as a catalytic agent to further agitate the already disturbed state of popular conscience. Important concessions granted by Walter of Brienne, dictator of the city of Florence in 1342–1343, to *il popolo minuto* had stimulated the revolutionary ardor of this class. The workers now demanded rights and privileges that formerly had been the exclusive prerogative of the upper classes.

SOURCE. Marvin Becker, "Florentine Politics and the Diffusion of Heresy in the Trecento—a Socioeconomic Inquiry," *Speculum* XXXIV (1959), pp. 67–75. Reprinted by permission of the publisher.

Ultimately they sought to justify these claims in terms of the prevailing "heretical" ethic. Their newly acquired sense of importance was heightened when they discerned that the oligarchs were dependent upon their assistance to effectuate the overthrow of the tyranny of Brienne. The doctrine of the Fraticelli further reinforced the confidence of *il popolo minuto* by ascribing the highest virtues to the poor.

By the end of the Trecento the problem of heresy had become peripheral and the Signoria was no longer obliged to take cognizance of its existence. The oligarchical regime in power at this time had been able to eradicate its overt manifestations among *il popolo minuto* and in this effort they were aided by the fact that this particular class had become politically apathetic. Contemporary intellectual developments, with their emphasis upon philology and history and their tendency to ignore this controversial question in favor of secular studies, also contributed towards the waning of the influence of the teachings of the Fraticelli. No longer were anonymous chronicles in evidence which exhibited Franciscan overtones of sympathy for the plight of the lower classes. Finally, the fact that the humanist historical tradition was intensely hostile to the participation of the lower orders in communal life and opposed any force that might tend to agitate the conscience of *il popolo minuto* was a further deterrent to the diffusion of this heresy.

The absence of a satisfactory synthetic history on the subject of religious life in Trecento Italy and the fact that only three volumes of the records of the inquisition (dating from the sixteenth century) are to be found in the state archives of Florence, tends to make the establishment of general conclusions extremely tenuous. It might be fair to suggest, however, based upon Florentine historical experience, that the diffusion of heresy was intimately related to political considerations—just as its suppression ultimately stemmed from the same source.

33   *The Analysis of Collective Behavior*

Neil Smelser, author of Theory of Collective Behavior, *indicates some of the sophisticated sociological methods of understanding medieval religious behavior. If one*

SOURCE. Neil J. Smelser, *Theory of Collective Behavior* (London: Routledge & Kegan Paul Ltd.; New York: The Macmillan Company, 1962), pp. 12–15, 175–176, 187–188. Reprinted by permission of the publishers.

asked, for example, why religious disaffection never went as far as a Protestant revolt during the Middle Ages, one might conclude that there was, in Smelser's terms, little structural conduciveness.

THE DETERMINANTS OF COLLECTIVE BEHAVIOR

The Organization of Determinants. So far we have attempted to establish outside limits and internal divisions for the field of collective behavior. Explanation raises a different set of issues: What determines whether an episode of collective behavior *of any sort* will occur? What determines whether one type *rather than another* will occur? Many of the existing answers to these questions are unsatisfactory scientifically. As Strauss has observed, many students of panic have failed to distinguish any specific and determinate set of conditions for the occurrence of panic above and beyond a simple list of possibly operative factors:

"The conditions of panic can be roughly classified into three categories: physiological, psychological, and sociological. Physiological factors are fatigue, under-nourishment, lack of sleep, toxic conditions of the body, and the like. Psychological factors are surprise, uncertainty, anxiety, feeling of isolation, consciousness or powerlessness before the inevitable expectancy of danger. Sociological factors include lack of group solidarity, crowd conditions, lack of regimental leadership in the group. An effective statement of the mechanics of panic causation cannot be made by merely listing the factors entering into that causation when these factors are as diverse in character as they seem to be. A student seeking a genuinely effective statement of panic causation would attempt to find what is essential to these diverse conditions and tie these essential conditions into a dynamic statement of the development and outbreak of the panic occurrence."

These determinants must be organized. Each must be assigned to its appropriate contributory role in the genesis of panic. A mere list will not suffice.

Even more, we must organize the determinants precisely enough so that panic is the *only* possible outcome; we must rule out related outbursts. To quote Strauss again,

". . . the conditions of panic which have been noted, because they are not genuine causative conditions, are conditions for more than panic.

That is to say, the conditions for panic which are listed in the literature are not conditions for panic specifically; they are also conditions for other kinds of closely related phenomena. . . . The thin line between the occurrence of panic and the occurrence of . . . other types of non-rational behavior is attested to by the rapid shifts from one of these forms to another in battle—from collective exaltation to panic, from panic to collective fascination, and the like.

"In a genuine sense, then, the causes for panic are not specific causes. They are also conditions for other types of collective behavior."

We need, then, a *unique* combination of determinants which yields a *unique* outcome, panic. We must systematize the determinants, and note the changes in the combinations of determinants which produce different outcomes.

Similar problems of explanation arise in connection with social movements. In examining the anthropological literature on messianic movements, Barber concludes that there exists a "positive correlation of the messianic movement and deprivation [of various types]." The first difficulty in attempting to assess this correlation—assuming that it exists—is that "deprivation is a vague term. A statement of the kinds of deprivation is necessary. In addition, there are many types of messianic movements; some are associated with a positive sense of regeneration of society, others with passive resignation. Finally, as Barber notes, messianism is not the only response to deprivation; among "several alternative responses" he mentions "armed rebellion and physical violence" and "depopulation." Thus, in spite of Barber's correlation, there remain several kinds and levels of deprivation and several responses besides messianism. This is what we mean when we say that there exists a residue of indeterminacy in the connections between determinants and outcomes in the field of collective behavior. To reduce this residue is one of the major tasks of this study.

The Logic of Value-added.   The scheme we shall use to organize the determinants of collective behavior resembles the conception of "value-added" in the field of economics. An example of the use of this term is the conversion of iron ore into finished automobiles by a number of stages of processing. Relevant stages would be mining, smelting, tempering, shaping, and combining the steel with other parts, painting, delivering to retailer, and selling. Each stage "adds its value" to the final cost of the finished product. The key element in this example is that the earlier stages must combine *according to a certain pattern* before the next stage can contribute its particular value to the finished product. It is impossible to paint iron ore and hope that the painting will thereby contribute to the desired final product, an automobile. Painting, in order to be effective as a "determinant" in shaping the product, has to "wait" for the completion of the earlier processes. Every stage in the value-added process, therefore, is a necessary condition for the appropriate and effective addition of value in the next stage. The sufficient condition for final production, moreover, is the combination of *every* necessary condition, according to a definite pattern.

As the value-added process moves forward, it narrows progressively the range of possibilities of what the final product might become. Iron ore, for instance, is a very general resource, and can be converted into thousands of different kinds of products. After it is smelted and tempered into a certain quality of steel, the range of possible products into which it might enter is narrowed considerably. After it is pressed into automotive parts, it can be used for very few products other than automobiles. If we were to view the finished automobile as the "outcome" to be explained and the stages of value-added as "determinants," we would say that as each new stage adds its value, the "explanation" of the outcome becomes increasingly determinate or specific. As the value-added process develops, it allows for progressively fewer outcomes other than the one we wish to explain.

The logic of value-added can be applied to episodes of collective behavior, such as the panic or the reform movement. Many determinants, or necessary conditions, must be present for any kind of collective episode to occur. These determinants must combine, however, in a definite pattern. Furthermore, as they combine, the determination of the type of episode in question becomes increasingly specific, and alternative behaviors are ruled out as possibilities.

The following are the important determinants of collective behavior:

(1) Structural conduciveness. We read that financial booms and panics, fashion cycles and crazes do not plague simple, traditional societies; we also read that America as a civilization is prone to such seizures, and that, within America, places like Los Angeles and Detroit are especially productive of bizarre movements. Are such statements true, and if so, why? Do certain structural characteristics, more than others, permit or encourage episodes of collective behavior? To illustrate this condition of structural conduciveness with respect to the occurrence of financial panic, let us assume that prop-

erty is closely tied to kinship and can be transferred only to first-born sons at the time of the death of the father. Panic under such conditions is ruled out, simply because the holders of property do not have sufficient maneuverability to dispose of their assets upon short notice. Under conditions of economic pressure, certain responses are possible—for instance, a movement to change the customs of property transfer—but not panic. The structure of the social situation does not permit it. At the other extreme lies the money market, in which assets can be exchanged freely and rapidly.

Conduciveness is, at most, permissive of a given type of collective behavior. A money market, for instance, even though its structure is conducive to panic, may function for long periods without producing a crisis. Within the scope of a conducive structure, many possible kinds of behavior other than panic remain. We must narrow the range of possibilities. In order to do so, we add several more determinants. In this way we make more probable the occurrence of that event (e.g., panic) which is merely possible within the scope of conduciveness.

[In his section on the craze, Smelser continues to discuss structural conduciveness.]

STRUCTURAL CONDUCIVENESS

Previously we have shown that conditions of structural conduciveness for panic include the possibility of danger, withdrawal, and communication. Sometimes these conditions arise unexpectedly (e.g., in the case of encirclement on a battlefield); sometimes, however, conduciveness is institutionalized (e.g., in the case of the definition of exchange in the money market). In the latter case conduciveness is part of the normal definition of the social situation. In the study of crazes we can observe these conducive institutional conditions very clearly.

General Conditions of Conductiveness.   Four structural conditions are necessary if any craze is to appear:

(1) A structurally differentiated setting for social action. Structural differentiation refers to the level of specialization of a given kind of action (e.g., economic), and the degree to which specialized sanctions (money, in this case) are allowed to operate without intervention of other kinds of sanctions (e.g., political controls, kinship and other particularistic demands, etc.). An example of a highly differentiated economic structure is the market structure of the capitalist economies

of Great Britain and the United States in the nineteenth century, in which the norm was the pursuit of economic activity free from political interference and free from traditional loyalties to family and community. An example of an economic structure with a low degree of differentiation is the nuclear family, in which the allocation of economic resources is subordinated to the demands of the family as a unit (e.g., the demand that parent support children).

(2) A relatively well-defined "rationality" which governs the differentiated social action. People should be prepared to respond to specialized sanctions (e.g., money), and to make calculations in terms of maximizing their rewards. An example of this kind of rationality is the hypothetical "economic rationality" of classical economics, in which economic actors ignore all kinds of rewards except economic ones. An example of low economic rationality is the attitude of a person who refuses to maximize his income because in so doing he might hurt his family or friends.

(3) A possibility of committing, recommitting, and withdrawing resources with flexibility. In the economic sphere this involves a certain level of fluidity of capital.

(4) A "medium" which can be stored, exchanged, and extended to future commitments. Again in the economic sphere, money would be such a medium, perishable vegetables would not.

Let us illustrate these four general conditions of conduciveness in more detail in the economic, political, expressive, and religious spheres.

Conditions of Conduciveness in the Religious Sphere. Revivalism is a phenomenon primarily of the United States and Great Britain— countries with Anglo-Saxon, Protestant traditions. What kinds of religious settings characterize these countries, and how are these settings conducive to the occurrence of religious revivals?

(1) Differentiation of religious commitment. One of the major consequences of the Protestant Reformation was a redefinition of the basis of authority in society. The Protestants—with much variation among them—turned from the authority of a hierarchically ordered church to the reliance on an individual's relationship with God, with the Bible rather than the Church serving as the important inter-mediary. Structurally this brought differentiation—a split between the *religious* and the *political* authority of the church. For some time this split was not completed; many Protestant churches maintained a political fusion with the nation-state rather than the Papacy— Lutheranism in the German provinces and Scandinavia, Anglican-ism in England, and Presbyterianism in Scotland.

Later the fusion of Protestantism with political units began to give way to even more differentiated religious arrangements. The features of this development were the growth of Nonconformity in England and the separation of church and state in the American Constitution. In modern times a system of "denominational pluralism" has emerged, especially in the United States.

The religious outlook of some Protestant churches—especially Presbyterian, Congregationalist, Methodist, Baptist, and more recently, the Holiness branches—has developed in a way parallel to these lines of differentiation of religion from other spheres of society. Religious commitment, many within these churches have argued, should be a matter of voluntary choice based on faith, not a matter of being born into a church, being a citizen of a political unit, and so on. The voluntaristic position of these Protestant churches has been most conspicuous in their formative periods.

(2) Flexibility of religious commitment. Because of the voluntaristic definition of religious commitment in some branches of Protestantism, flexibility is increased. Church members can move from one denomination to another; they can, by emotional experience or personal choice, be "reborn" or "regenerated" without affecting their political citizenship, ascribed membership in a church, ethnic origin, etc. Hence evangelical Protestantism makes for a great fluidity of religious commitment.

(3) Commitment as "generalized medium." Religious belief thus becomes something that one can gain, lose, save and spend, according to the quality of one's personal conduct and faith. Other religions than evangelical Protestantism make such demands as well, but they impose these demands on top of an ascribed or semi-ascribed basis of inclusion.

(4) Religious rationality. In the evangelical branches of Protestantism, churches can be in the "business of saving souls" alone, and not concern themselves with political, economic, and social goals with which less differentiated churches invariably become entangled. Religious salvation, regeneration, and backsliding become more and more exclusively based on religious experience alone.

From a structural standpoint, then, the definition of the religious situation in the evangelical Protestant churches parallels that of a free market system, a system of open nomination of political candidates by convention, and an open stratification system. Within these churches we observe those features of differentiation, flexibility, and maneuverability that are conducive for crazelike behavior in general.

34   *Conclusion*

The following is drawn from Gordon Leff, Heresy in the Later Middle Ages.

_____

Ultimately, medieval heresy must be measured by its impact upon society. From the later twelfth century until the sixteenth century, it was continually combated by an increasing array of forces. But it was never overcome: and in the heresy of the Hussites, and to a lesser degree the English Lollards and the Waldensians, passed into the Reformation. Such a progression in one form or another was inherent in medieval society: on the one hand, heresy was an inevitable accompaniment of dissent in a world of orthodoxy; yet the very process of defining one in relation to the other narrowed the area in which heterodoxy could remain uncondemned. In that sense heresy was the outlet of a society with no outlets. Their absence made tensions into explosions, and common aspirations the programme of sects. Only when the latter became independent churches did heresy lose its impact. Instrumental in the crisis of the later medieval church, it waned with the waning of the church's ecumenicality. That was the paradox. Medieval heresy arose from within medieval society and declined with its supersession. It was a catholic phenomenon concerned with the universal issues confronting a catholic society. As such it must be treated.

NOTES TO PART VII

1. "Brüder des freien Geistes," *Realenzyklopädie für protestantische Theologie und Kirche*, 3d ed., vol. 3, 1897, p. 471.
2. Grundmann, *La mistica tedesca nei suoi reflessi popolari—il beghinismo. Relazioni del X. Congresso internazionale di scienze storiche*, III (Florence, 1955), 483.
3. Karl Marx, *Vorwort zur Kritik der politischen Ökonomie*, in Marx-Engels, *Ausgewählte Schriften in zwei Bändern* (Berlin, 1953), p. 338.
4. Friedrich Engels, *Der deutsche Bauernkrieg*, in *Marx-Engels-Lenin-Stalin zur deutschen Geschichte*, vol. 1. p. 203f.

SOURCE. Gordon Leff, *Heresy in the Later Middle Ages* (Manchester: Manchester University Press, 1967), p. 47. Reprinted by permission of the publisher and the author.

Bibliography

The following is a list of some of the best, most recent, or most readily available works relating to the study of medieval heresy. Works in English are given precedence, with only the most important works in foreign languages being included. Items available in paperback are starred with an asterisk.

I. WORKS ON CHURCH HISTORY IN GENERAL

*Geoffrey Barraclough, *The Medieval Papacy* (New York, 1968).

Jean Daniélou and Henri Marrou, *The Christian Centuries*, vol. 1: *The First Hundred Years* (London, 1964).

*Hans Jonas, *The Gnostic Religion* (Boston, 1963).

J. N. D. Kelly, *Early Christian Doctrines* (London, 1958).

Arnoldo Momigliano, *The Conflict Between Paganism and Christianity in the Fourth Century* (Oxford, 1963).

*David Knowles, *The Evolution of Medieval Thought* (Baltimore, 1962).

*Gordon Leff, *Medieval Thought—Saint Augustine to Ockham* (Baltimore, 1958).

*Jeffrey B. Russell, *A History of Medieval Christianity* (New York, 1968).

Julius R. Weinberg, *A Short History of Medieval Philosophy* (Princeton, 1964).

Until the completion of the *Christian Centuries* series, the best multivolume reference work on the history of the Church remains Augustin Fliche and Emile Martin, *Histoire de l'église* (Paris, Bloud and Gay), though this series has also not yet been completed.

II. WORKS ON HERESY AND DISSENT IN GENERAL; THE EARLY CHURCH; REFORMISM

Marvin B. Becker, "Florentine Politics and the Diffusion of Heresy in the Trecento: a Socioeconomic Inquiry," *Speculum*, XXIV (1959).

Christopher Brooke, "Heresy and Religious Sentiment, 1000–1250," *Bulletin of the Institute of Historical Research*, XLI (1968).

P. R. L. Brown, "Religious Dissent in the Later Roman Empire: the Case of North Africa," *History*, XLVI (1961).

*Norman Cohn, *The Pursuit of the Millennium* (London, 1957).

Antoine Dondaine, "Aux origines du valdéisme," *Archivium Fratrum Praedicatorum*, XVI (1946).

*James Fearns, *Ketzer und Ketzerbekämpfung im Hochmittelalter* (Göttingen, 1968).

W. H. C. Frend, *The Donatist Church: a Movement of Protest in Roman North Africa* (London, 1952).

George W. Greenaway, *Arnold of Brescia* (Cambridge, Eng., 1931).

S. L. Greenslade, *Schism in the Early Church* (London, 1964).

*Herbert Grundmann, *Ketzergeschichte des Mittelalters* (Göttingen, 1963).

Grundmann, "Ketzerverhöre des Spätmittelalters als quellenkritisches Problem," *Deutsches Archiv für die Erforschung des Mittelalters*, XXI (1965).

Grundmann, *Religiöse Bewegungen im Mittelalter*, 2d ed. (Hildesheim, 1961).

*Hans Jonas, *The Gnostic Religion: the Message of the Alien God and the Beginnings of Christianity* (Boston, 1958).

A. H. M. Jones, "Were Ancient Heresies National or Social Movements in Disguise?," *Journal of Theological Studies*, n.s., X (1959).

*Ronald Knox, *Enthusiasm* (Oxford, 1951).

Henry Charles Lea, *History of the Inquisition of the Middle Ages,* 3 vols. (New York, 1888). Last reprinted 1955.

Gordon Leff, *Heresy in the Later Middle Ages.* 2 vols. (Manchester, 1967).

R. I. H. Moore, "The Origins of Medieval Heresy," *History*, LV (1970).

Raffaello Morghen, *Medioevo cristiano*, 2d ed. (Bari, 1958).

Jeffrey Burton Russell, *Dissent and Reform in the Early Middle Ages* (Berkeley and Los Angeles, 1965).

Russell, "Interpretations of the Origins of Medieval Heresy," *Mediaeval Studies*, XXV (1963).

A. C. Shannon, *The Popes and Heresy in the Thirteenth Century* (New York, 1955).

L. Sommariva, "Studi recenti sulle eresie medioevali (1939–1952)," *Rivista storica italiana* (1952).

Christine Thouzellier, *Catharisme et Valdéisme en Languedoc, à la fin du XIIe et au début du XIIIe siècle* (Paris, 1966).

Thouzellier, *Hérésie et hérétiques* (Rome, 1969).

Walter Wakefield and Austin P. Evans, eds., *Heresies of the High Middle Ages* (New York, 1969).

Ernst Werner, *Pauperes Christi* (Berlin, 1956).

III. CATHARISM

Pierre de Berne-Lagarde, *Bibliographie du Catharisme Languedocien* (Toulouse, 1957).

Arno Borst, *Die Katharer* (Stuttgart, 1953).

Antoine Dondaine, "Les actes du concile albigeois de Saint-Félix de Caraman," *Miscellanea Giovanni Mercati*, vol. 5 (*Studi e Testi* No. 125).

Dondaine, "Nouvelles sources de l'histoire doctrinale du néomanichéisme du moyen âge," *Revue de Sciences Philosophiques et Theologiques*, XXVIII (1939).

Dondaine, *Un traité néomanichéen du XIIIe siècle* (Rome, 1939).

Dondaine, "L'hiérarchie cathare en Italie," *Archivium Fratrum Praedicatorum,* XIX (1949) and XX (1950).

Richard W. Emery, *Heresy and Inquisition in Narbonne* (New York, 1941).

Dmitri Obolensky, *The Bogomils, A Study in Balkan Neomanichaeism* (Cambridge, Eng. 1948).

Steven Runciman, *The Medieval Manichee* (Cambridge, Eng. 1947).

Daniel Walther, "A Survey of Recent Research on the Albigensian Cathari," *Church History,* XXXIV (1965).

IV. INTELLECTUAL HERESIES

Morton W. Bloomfield, "Joachim of Flora," *Traditio,* XIII (1957).

Allan J. Macdonald, *Berengar and the Reform of Sacramental Doctrine* (London, Longmans Green, 1930).

Edward J. Martin, *A History of the Iconoclastic Controversy* (London, 1930).

J. G. Sikes, *Peter Abailard* (Cambridge, Eng., 1932).

V. LATE MEDIEVAL HERESY AND THE REFORMATION

Margaret Aston, "Lollardy and the Reformation: Survival or Revival? *History,* XLIX (1964).

Margaret Deanesley, *The Lollard Bible* (Cambridge, Eng., 1920).

Decima L. Douie, *The Nature and the Effect of the Heresy of the Fraticelli* (Manchester, 1932).

Claus Peter Clasen, "Medieval Heresies in the Reformation," *Church History,* XXXII (1963).

Gordon Leff, "Heresies and the Decline of the Medieval Church," *Past and Present,* No. 20 (1961).

*K. B. McFarlane, *The Origins of Religious Dissent in England* (New York, 1966; first published as *John Wycliffe and the Beginnings of English Nonconformity,* New York, 1953).

J. A. F. Thomson, *The Later Lollards,* 1414–1520 (London, 1965).

Matthew Spinka, ed., *John Hus at the Council of Constance* (New York, 1965).

J. Ancelet-Hustache, *Master Eckhart and Rhineland Mysticism* (London, 1959).

Joseph Dahmus, *The Prosecution of John Wyclif* (New Haven, 1952).

Matthew Spinka, *John Hus and the Czech Reform* (Chicago, 1941).

H. B. Workman, *John Wyclif,* 2 vols. (Oxford, 1926).